The Making of Joel and E...
The Big Lebowski

The Making of Joel and Ethan Coen's

The Big Lebowski

Edited by Tricia Cooke

Text by William Preston Robertson

Illustrations by John Todd Anderson and Rafael Sañudo

faber and faber

First published in the United States in 1998
by W.W. Norton & Company Inc.
500 Fifth Avenue, New York, New York 10110

First published in the United Kingdom in 1998
by Faber and Faber Limited
3 Queen Square London WC1N 3AU

Printed in England by Clays Ltd, St Ives plc

Extracts from the screenplay of *The Big Lebowski* © 1998 Ethan Coen and Joel Coen
Portions of this work by William Preston Robertson have appeared in *American Film,*
Playboy and *Twin Cities Reader*

William Preston Robertson, Tricia Cooke, John Todd Anderson and Rafael Sanudo are
hereby identified as authors of this work in accordance with Section 77 of the
Copyright, Designs and Patents Act 1988

A CIP record for this book
is available from the British Library

ISBN 0–571–19334–X

10 9 8 7 6 5 4 3 2 1

For my parents, John and Patti Cooke.

—T.C.

Dedicated to my mother, the great historian, Mary Demmond Robertson, and my father, the great physician, Mason Gordon Robertson. They're pretty good parents, too.

—W.P.R.

Acknowledgments

or their help in making this book I would like to thank J. Todd
nderson, Karen Anonia, Alex Belth, Amy Cherry, Ethan Coen,
ɔel Coen, Dan Conaway, Roger Deakins, David Diliberto, Julia
ruskin, Eric Fellner, Jay Floyd, Rick Heinrichs, Sydney Lunn,
ɔanne Muellmann, Pat Murphy, Nancy Palmquist, Bill Robertson,
afael Sañudo, Jennifer Scanlon, Alan Schoolcraft, Caroline
ɔuthey, Nomi Victor, Chris Welch, and Mary Zophres.

—Tricia Cooke

would like to thank J. Todd Anderson, Jody Podolsky, and Karen
achs, each of whom generously provided me with shelter during

my stay in Los Angeles. Thanks also to Gregg Edler, Tom Elkins, Kimberly Rach, and Marty Houston in *The Big Lebowski*'s front office for their endless help and indefatigable good humor (well, at any rate, they never failed to laugh at my jokes). Thanks to Pat Murphy, who taught me, among other things, the word "asymptotic." Thanks, too, to my dear friend Trish Cooke, who shared a little dream and in so doing gave me the opportunity to pull together over ten years' worth of imbecilic writing on the Coens.

Very special thanks go to my beloved wife (another great physician), Claire Pomeroy, whose support, pride, patience, and forgiveness during the writing of this book made it possible.

And finally, my thanks to Joel for making Fran a woman (oops, wrong thank-you speech). And to Ethan, whose friendship through the years has been one of my life's profoundly entertaining pleasures.

—William Preston Robertson

Contents

The Making of The Big Lebowski

had a memorable phone conversation with the boss on the sofa.

Introduction

*I*t was several months after Joel and Ethan Coen's most ambitiously stylistic and expensive movie to date, *The Hudsucker Proxy* (1994), had taken the nation by—well, by a storm of sorts, blowing loudly and swiftly through theaters from which most customers beat a screaming retreat, that I had a memorable phone conversation with the boys on the subject of their next film.

Those were dark times indeed. With *Hudsucker,* the Coens felt they had taken an earnest shot at making a commercially viable, "Hollywood" movie (a questionable if not laughable assessment, but here you have it), only to see the movie bomb even more catastrophically than the movie that was previously their most ambi-

Joel and Ethan with producer Graham Place during the filming of *The Hudsucker Proxy*.

tiously stylistic and expensive to date, *Miller's Crossing* (1990). Joel and Ethan were contemplating, with considerable ill ease, just what the point of things was—you know: moviemaking-wise.

The broad artistic license the movie industry had granted them for so many years in the hope that such patience might someday be rewarded with a box-office hit in addition to a merely critical one was, the Coen brothers believed, swiftly narrowing. The clock was ticking. The heat was on. As was the pressure. The movie industry was standing with its pin-striped arms crossed over its carnation-adorned lapel, tapping its wingtipped shoe, occasionally sighing heavily through its nostrils and checking its pocket watch.

What were the Coens to do? Try harder to sell out? Walk a bit farther away from their funky, offbeat cave into the sunlight of obviousness and accessibility? Or just say the hell with it and retreat deeper into the cave, to communicate with ever fewer people by means of ever more obscure batlike shrieks?

Being reasonably canny men, they chose—

The latter.

"Jesus Christ!" I bellowed into the phone when they called t share their good news. "I implore you, as your friend who cares about you and wants to see you do well in life, don't make *Fargo!* It's the weirdest, most bizarre, most inaccessible of all of the things you've written! You're retreating into—" And here, I recounted the whole cave analogy. "Listen to me," I said. "Even your most diehard fans aren't going to know what to make of *Fargo!* You're whittling down your audience from the already marginal subset of egghead art-house moviegoers to only the members of that subset who live in or are familiar with upstate Minnesota! You're making this movie for a demographic of seven people, tops! And what if one of them is sick or out of town when your movie opens?"

They responded with a syncopated duet of strangulated, spasmodic laughter. They almost sounded proud.

I was galled. "Do not make *Fargo!*" I intoned. "It's career suicide! Do not make *Fargo!*"

I recalled that phone exchange with Joel and Ethan as I sat with a plate of pasta on pinched knees in the living room of costume designer Mary Zophres's bungalow, while a small crowd of movie

Joel and Ethan in the Dude's bungalow.

The Coens Oeuvre-Easy

A Handy Guide to Coen Motifs

As a service to film buffs, teachers, critics, and other species of pedant, we present here a synopticon of the motifs with which the Coens most frequently window-dress their cinematic efforts. Essentially there are six recurring motifs:(1) howling fat men, (2) blustery titans, (3) vomiting, (4) violence, (5) dreams, and (6) peculiar haircuts. Occasionally, a doctoral student in film criticism will suggest "hats—the losing and putting back on of," as a seventh motif. Should you encounter such a person, point out that the "lost hat" theme has appeared definitively in only two Coen movies, and frankly, you're not sure whether it's a legitimate motif or just some cheap joke. (So you'll know what you're talking about, however, "lost hat" data is included here when valid.)

Blood Simple. Howling Fat Man: M. Emmet Walsh, upon getting his

industry people obscured my view of a rented wide-screen television set in a sudden frenzy of jumping, clapping, and ululating, because Joel had just paid them tribute in his acceptance speech for Best Original Screenplay Oscar. For *Fargo.*

As stylishly garbed crewfolk jounced amiably around me—Joel and Ethan's flat, three-foot-tall faces now and then peeking out between them—I examined anew, and not without some bemusement, the cognitive path that had led me to attempt to dissuade the boys from making what I now had to think of as a 1997 Academy Award–winning career suicide.

But it was so much weirder even than that. *Fargo* wasn't just a mainstream award-winner. It was the most financially successful movie the Coens had ever made.

The truth is, Joel and Ethan themselves were blindsided by *Fargo*'s success. The Coen brothers are quiet men by nature—spare of words, uncomfortable with social fuss. And in the weeks prior to the Academy Awards, two more miserable-looking creatures had hand kebobbed to the windowsill of an adjacent room by Frances McDormand. Blustery Titan: Dan Hedaya, as Marty the bar owner, is not a blustery titan in the classic sense, but he is the only person in the movie who owns property, and he does boss people around a bit. A blustery titan prototype. Vomiting: Dan Hedaya is dyspeptic and/or nauseated for most of his scenes, a condition that bears fruit, as it were, three times—once off-screen, when shown alleged "corpse" photos of Frances McDormand and John Getz, then twice on-screen, when Fran kicks him in the groin during an attempted rape and during a dream sequence of hers in which he upchucks the local blood bank's entire inventory. Violence: Yes. Dreams: See aforementioned regurgitated blood bank bit. Peculiar Haircuts: None this time, perhaps due to budgetary concerns. Lost Hats: After howling, then shooting holes in a wall and punching his fist through it to unstake the knife in his hand, M. Emmet calmly pauses to pick up his hat and don it.

never trod the earth's crust, as well-wishers regularly dropped by the Los Angeles set of their latest movie to bask in the boys' karmic glow. There was the seemingly endless stream of awards banquets they had to attend: the Directors Guild Awards, the Writers Guild Awards, the Producers Guild Awards, the Golden Globes, and the Independent Spirit Awards. And then, on those occasions when they actually won something and had to go to the podium to speak—oh! how pathetically miserable they were.

It was as though the Coens' cruel and quirky cinematic universe had sprung a leak into their real lives and turned the boys into unwitting characters in one of their own movies: two independent filmmakers intentionally try to make a commercial movie and it bombs; they turn around, make an intentionally inaccessible movie, and suddenly they're laughing, slapping backs, and chatting it up with Joan Rivers on E!

As Joel stepped from the podium, Mary Zophres shushed the room. On TV, Ethan had now stepped up to the mike, gold statuette

> *Raising Arizona.* Howling Fat Men: John Goodman and William Forsythe, upon discovering as they drive down the highway that they have left Gale/Nathan Jr. behind at the scene of a bank robbery, and for quite some time after that. Blustery Titan: Trey Wilson as the curmudgeon with a heart of gold, Nathan Arizona, owner of "Unpainted Arizona" furniture stores and progenitor of the Arizona Quints. Vomiting: Not this time, though there is quite a bit of mouth drool both from the babies and from Tex Cobb, the Wart Hog from Hell. Violence: Yes. Dreams: Hi has them throughout, encountering everything from Tex Cobb, the Wart Hog from Hell, to Nathan Jr. as a teenaged football hero, to Hi and Edwina as doting grandparents. Peculiar Haircuts: And how. Nicolas Cage's Woody Woodpecker do, Gale and Evelle Snopes's Brillcreamed bouffants, and more.
>
> *Miller's Crossing.* Howling Fat Man: Mario Tedesco as Drop Johnson, upon witnessing Jon Polito whacking J. E. Freeman in the face with a fireplace shovel. Blustery Titan: Jon Polito as the ambitious, ethics-

in hand, and mumbled in what would have been a drone had it not been so disrupted by halting, pressured inhalations, two emotionally disassociative sentences, the subject of one of which, I think, was "Billy Bob and the other nominees." Then, his effusion reservoir apparently drained, he turned and shambled offstage, the orchestra playing incongruously stirring music in his wake.

I looked down, stabbed my pasta. Nope. Nothing wrong with my logic. *Fargo* was the most inaccessible movie the Coens had made. That the American public perversely chose to go see it and then recommend the movie to their friends was beside the point. My thinking was sound.

Still, the day after the Oscars, I put the question to Ethan. "I was right to advise you against doing *Fargo*, wasn't I? I mean, as friend."

It was a good day for the Coens. Both of them were looking more chipper than I'd seen them in a while. Indeed, they were radiant-not with pride at winning, but with that special kind of relief see

conscious, psychopathic, blow-hard gang boss, Johnny Caspar. Vomiting: Gabriel Byrne tosses the barley twice, the first time off-screen as a result of a post-poker-game hangover, the second time on-screen as he is being led to Miller's Crossing, where he thinks he will be killed. Violence: Yes. Dreams: Gabriel Byrne has a recurring one about losing his hat. In fact, the movie's title sequence opens with a lovely pas de fedora, as his windblown lid bounces in slow-motion through a forest glade. Peculiar Haircuts: Hoo boy, are there ever. Being a period gangster picture, everyone, with the exception of leading man Gabriel Byrne, has that shaved-back-of-the-head-with-the-slicked-down-mat-of-hair-on-top, pink-scrubbed-jug-eared-Hitler Youth look so in vogue in the '30s. Lost Hats: Without even including the oneiric fedora, this film would still represent the apotheosis of the Coens' brief flirtation with lost headgear, as Gabriel Byrne repeatedly loses his and puts it back on throughout the movie.

(continued)

in the faces of men at the doctor's office who know that the scrotal examination part of their physical is over.

"Sure," Ethan said, beaming.

I had the feeling that Ethan would agree with anything I said that day. He was of an agreeable mind; he was hoisting his britches and fastening his belt buckle, emotionally speaking.

I pressed further. "Have you learned anything from the experience?" I asked impishly. "Now that you know the winning formula, are you going to quit making inaccessible movies like *Fargo* and focus on more conventional fare so as to avoid this kind of unrelenting success in the future?"

Ethan hyperventilated through his nostrils, which the Coens will do when they are only mildly amused. He shrugged, lifted his hand up, then dropped it to his knee. "What're you going to do, you know? I mean, if a movie like *Fargo* succeeds, then clearly nothing much makes sense, and so, you know, you might as well make whatever kind of movie you want and hope for the best."

Barton Fink. Howling Fat Man: John Goodman again, during the climactic "burning hallway" sequence. Blustery Titan: Michael Lerner, as Jack Lipnik, the head of Capitol Pictures, a cross between Nathan Arizona and Johnny Caspar—affable, and yet a psycho. Vomiting: Twice. John Mahoney, as alcoholic Southern novelist turned Hollywood scriptwriter W. P. Mayhew, in a bathroom stall, upon Barton's first meeting him, and John Goodman, when he staggers into Barton's bathroom upon seeing Judy Davis's murdered stiff. Violence: Yes. Dreams: Depending on your interpretation, the entire movie. Peculiar Haircuts: Again, it's a period picture, so there's some whitewalling around the ears, but the undeniable tonsorial standout here is Barton's majestic Chariot of the Gods coif. Lost Hats: In the original script, during burning-hallway sequence, Pete the elevator operator (Harry Bugin) staggers out into the hall, clutching his head, then collapses to the floor, and his head rolls off. A possible contender for the motif, if your understanding of "hat" is loose enough. The head-rolling scene was actually filmed, but never used because of technical problems.

I nodded. I wasn't sure what we were talking about anymore. "So, I'm right. *Fargo* was career suicide."

"Sure," Ethan nodded.

The Coen brothers were born in Minnesota (Joel in 1954 and Ethan in 1957) and exhibit that region's economy of speech and resistance to overt displays of emotion. Joel is lanky, dark-haired, and ponytailed. In his more pensive moments, he will sit slouched in a chair with an expression that resembles an afghan catching the faint scent of game in the wind. Ethan is somewhat shorter, but has a large, fuzzier head, and, in his more pensive moments, exhibits a propensity for tireless, outside-the-delivery-room-style pacing. The lack of contention between the two suggests either rare unity of vision or common Midwestern reserve.

Their shared sense of humor is an impossible mix of offbeat, free-range intellectualism, slapstick of both the physical and metaphy

The Hudsucker Proxy. Howling Fat Man: The suicidal though graceful Charles Durning as he swan-dives the length of the Hudsucker Industries building. Blustery Titan: Paul Newman as Mussburger, the evil genius behind the imbecile Norville Barnes's promotion. Vomiting: Tim Robbins's chicken à la king seeks daylight after he carries the swooning Jennifer Jason Leigh up the fire stairs of the Hudsucker Industries building to his office on the top floor. Violence: Yes. Dreams: Tim Robbins has a dreamscape ballet with ephemerally garbed loveliness vision Pamela Everett, who represents either Success, Hope, Norville's creative Muse, or Joel Silver's back-end Profits. Peculiar Haircuts: Relatively muted this time out. Norville has a chuckle-brained, tousle-haired look, but I'm not convinced Tim Robbins didn't come to the role with his hair already like that. From there, the funny-hair banner is picked up by secondary characters Buzz, the bristle-beaned Elevator Gnat (Jim True), and Mussburger's bun-surmounted secretary (Mary Lou Rosato).

(continued)

cal type, extremely subtle irony, extremely obvious irony, idiotic, repetitive wordplay, and a weakness for silly haircuts.

Their taste in filmmakers is similarly catholic, ranging from Kurosawa to Preston Sturges to whoever made Bob Hope's *I'll Take Sweden*. Their own movies are, depending on your taste, either admirably bold or ludicrously misguided attempts to reconcile these influences.

Cerebral one minute, slaphappy the next, they are set in a chaotic yet oddly predetermined universe. Their movies are Postmodern Tales of Everyman exploring the proposition that we are all more or less imbeciles at one time or another. The recurrent motifs around which they build these explorations are themselves the stuff of madness and chaos: violence, bellowing, obesity, vomiting, lost hats, dreams. But the manner in which the chaos is presented is as precise and clean and certain as that in any movie made during Hollywood's Golden Age.

Their movies have a clearly recognizable look: wide-angle lenses that carefully frame complex action; swiftly kinetic camera move-

Fargo. **Howling Fat Man: None.** Though Frances McDormand as Marge Gunderson is pregnant, she refrains from howling. **Blustery Titan:** Harve Presnell as hale, hardy family patriarch Wade "No Jean, No Money" Gustafson. **Vomiting:** While inspecting a murder scene, the pregnant, morning-sickness-besieged Frances McDormand must squat until the urge to vomit passes. **Violence: Yes. Dreams: None,** though not for lack of trying on the Coens' part. An early script draft included an uninspired dream sequence for Marge involving Native Amer-ican imagery and a fetus. The scene was dropped when the boys could not agree on a spelling for "foetus." **Peculiar Haircuts: None,** though peculiar hats abound. **Lost Hats:** Now, see, this proves that the whole Lost Hat thing is bogus, because this is a hat movie if there ever was one—and not a single hat gets lost. Not Frances McDormand's Red Square Reviewing Stand number, not Peter Stormare's little Laplander, not William Macy's Tyrolean Bourgeois. It seems to me that if the Coens were really serious about the motif,

ments; unsettling camera angles born partly from the disturbed malevolence of film noir, partly from the wacky, elastic physical laws of Looney Toons cartoons.

Joel, the older, directs. Ethan, the younger, produces.

And vice versa.

Except for the older, younger part.

They write their screenplays together, alternating the order of their names from script to script.

And they edit the end product together—quaintly, with grease pencil and film, using the pseudonym Roderick Jaynes.

One might easily expect them to sleep in bed together, wearing nightshirts and nightcaps and contrapuntally snoring, à la Laurel and Hardy.

But they do not.

So, who are they? What is the secret behind their career? How for crying out loud, do they manage to make inaccessible movie that people will—sometimes, anyway—actually pay to see?

To understand the men, we must understand the artists.

this would have been the movie in which to show it.

The Big Lebowski. Howling Fat Man: John Goodman, the Coens' all-time favorite HFM, goes for best three out of four as the irrepressible, gun-waving, Corvette-bashing Walter Sobchak. Blustery Titan: David Huddleston as the pompous and paraplegic millionaire Big Lebowski. Vomiting: None, though John Goodman does spit out part of a nihilist's ear. Violence: Yes. Dreams: This movie boasts two major dream set pieces, one of which is a musical dance extravaganza for the entire family, featuring a Busby Berkeley–style chorus line, Saddam Hussein, early Kenny Rogers "drug" music, and more. Peculiar Haircuts: Jeff Bridges, as Jeff "Dude" Lebowski, has a kind of Samurai-relaxing-at-home look for his shoulder-length hair, pinning the front locks back in an upper-tier ponytail while the remaining locks hang; John Goodman wears a flattop; and John Turturro, as the Dude and Walters' pederastic bowling nemesis Quintana, wears a hairnet. ∎

understand the artists, we must understand the art. And to understand the art, we must examine the process. But to examine the process . . .

We must go back . . . back . . . to St. Louis Park, Minnesota, in the late '60s, when that Minneapolis suburb was mostly undeveloped swampland, and Joel and kid brother Ethan were members of a small tribe of skinny Jewish kids with fantastically overgrown hair, lounging on the sofa of Ed and Rena Coen's basement den, bored beyond comprehension. An idea occurred to Joel of how to relieve the chest-squeezing tedium of their meaningless teenage lives: super 8mm home movies.

The plan was to mow neighborhood lawns and thereby raise enough capital to purchase a movie camera and film stock. Ron Neter—today a commercial producer in Los Angeles—was a principal architect of the scheme. Says Neter: "The hardest part—we'd lined up all these customers—was convincing Joel to, you know, get up and mow the lawns. He needed a big pep talk to get up and do it."

Whatever tonic Neter used in his pep, it worked, because eventually they bought a Vivitar camera and some film. Now they had to decide what to shoot. To this end, they headed back to Ed and Rena's basement den.

Their earliest explorations were, to be sure, uninspired, if not disgracefully lazy. Setting the movie camera up in front of the television, they simply let it run—filming, at least in part, a Raymond Burr jungle movie. It was an act of artistic lethargy that shamed even the boys, and they soon carted the Vivitar outdoors to see what might be worth filming there. On one occasion, they filmed their sneakered feet down the length of their own legs as they descended a slide. On another occasion, Joel lay on his back beneath a tree, pointed the Vivitar skyward, and filmed neighborhood youths jumping from the tree down around him. Such forays proved only marginally less disappointing than the Raymond Burr movie, and they soon realized that what they needed was actors. Enter Mark Zimmering—a.k.a. Zeimers—and, for the Coens, the greatest period of creative productivity in their Super 8mm career. Mark Zimmering was an exuberant youth with a shock of dark, Brillo-y hair, garish orthodontic braces, a shit-eating grin, and, most important, an eagerness to run over to the Coens' house and leap enthusiastically before the camera at a moment's notice.

"Uh, I don't know. I guess I was the—probably, I was the—I don't know," says Dr. Mark Zimmering, today a distinguished endocrinologist. "I was the one with the most charisma, I guess."

If Zeimers was their Robert De Niro, then Ethan, with his black framed Buddy Holly glasses and his reddish Judeo-Rastafarian corona of hair, became Harvey Keitel. Ethan was a mere wisp physically and thus could be lifted and hurled across the room with ease if the scene required it—and even if it didn't. He also could fit more easily into his sister Debbie's tutu, a beloved semiregular prop.

The Super 8s from the Zeimers Years represent a serendipitous merging of the star's unique thespian stylings with the Coens' earliest filmmaking impulses. Which is to say they involve a lot of foc mugging and are rip-offs of things seen on television.

Among the best of the lot is *Zeimers in Zambezi*, a remake of the 66 Cornel Wilde movie *The Naked Prey*. Zeimers, fully clothed and eed sporting a fuzzy winter hat with earflaps, is the Cornel Wilde rogate, while Ethan is the angrily bellowing native who, waving pear and sporting Buddy Holly glasses, pursues Zeimers in a entless cat-and-mouse chase. Also worthy of mention is *Ed . . . a* ʒ, a remake of the 1943 tearjerker *Lassie Come Home*, thoughtfully dated to mirror the generational turmoil of the '60s. Zeimers ets and bonds with Ed, a dog, and asks his parents if he can keep n. He is met with blustery rejection from both the father, played Ron Neter, and the mother, who, in the finest of Elizabethan the- ical traditions, is played by Ethan, shown sitting on the sofa, aring Debbie's tutu, inexplicably banging on a drum set. Zeimers mptly lifts Ethan up and hurls him across the room with ease. ter, cowed, now acquiesces in a style of acting reminiscent of the ito. The film ends on an upbeat note, with Zeimers turning vard the camera to deliver his trademark metallic, shit-eating n.

Joel and Ethan with costume designer Richard Hornung.

But the pinnacle of the Coens' Super 8 years is a little masterpiece called *The Banana Film*. Shot in a Godardian hand-held cinema verité style, and originally intended to be viewed while Frank Zappa's *Hot Rats* album was played along, *The Banana Film* was one of the Coens' last Zeimers films.

Now showing his age, but no longer his braces, Zeimers plays a hip, happy-go-lucky Samaritan with a consuming passion for, and a superhuman ability to olfactorially detect, bananas. After a brief opening sequence the story shifts to Ethan. Adorned for the last time on screen in Debbie's tutu, Ethan is shown hurled out the front door of his house into the snow, a shovel following close behind. Ethan staggers to his feet, begins slavishly shoveling the walk, and soon has a heart attack and dies. Zeimers comes across Ethan's lifeless body. Then he smells something. Rifling the fallen shoveler's pockets, Zeimers uncovers a banana. With this, he continues on his way, inhaling and eating his treasure.

At this point, the film makes a hairpin turn into destiny. Zeimers stops in his tracks, clutches his stomach, gazes alarmedly into the camera, and introduces a motif that has appeared in almost every Coen movie created since: he vomits.

"It was in a bowl," Ron Neter states flatly. "They took a lot of great pain and care into mixing the different ingredients. And then they showed him from behind, retching. It poured from the bowl onto the ground so quickly, it's just a blur. But Joel and Ethan liked the consistency of it, so we did this long, lingering close-up."

Here, Neter pauses to reflect on what the scene represents in the Coens' body of work. "They really have had an affinity for vomit in their films, I guess. On *Miller's Crossing,* I remember a lot of discussion, particularly with the special effects department—you know, saying that Tom didn't eat much, he just drank a lot, so his vomit had to be very runny. I think they were ultimately disappointed with the results. But Joel and Ethan entertained these kinds of conversations with a lot of, you know, attention."

Eventually, Joel left Minnesota for Simon's Rock, a private college in the Berkshires of Massachusetts, then later New York University film school. Ethan was left to experiment with his own solo efforts. He conceived of a film called *Froggy Went a Courtin'*. It would be an artful montage of run-over toads, with a recording of Odetta singing the title song in the background. But Ethan could find no squashed toads, and soon he too left Minnesota for Simon's Rock, then Princeton, where he studied philosophy.

He would not pick up a camera again until *Blood Simple*.

My own first exposure to the boys' extraordinary filmmaking skills in action occurred in the summer of 1983, when I stopped off to visit Joel and Ethan in New York while driving home from graduate school in a Honda leprous with rust and sagging with my earthly possessions.

Joel and Ethan were in the editing stages of a movie we all felt certain was their first important step in what would eventually become a highly successful career making feature films for some of the more remote drive-in theaters in Mississippi, playing double-bill undercard to Jesse Vint movies. The Coens had a title for their movie, but they knew eventually it would have to be changed, since no movie executive in his right mind would retain a title as idiotic as *Blood Simple*—a term they had lifted from the pages of Dashiell Hammett's *Red Harvest* in what would be the first of many such moochings.

It was a movie that had been born, conceptually, when Ethan was working as a temp office clerk at Macy's and Joel as an assistant editor on a budget horror movie called *The Evil Dead*. Sam Raimi, *The Evil Dead*'s young director (and director since of *Darkman* and *The Quick and the Dead*), shared the Coens' fascination with what one might call "projectile cinema," and told them of his patented "shaky cam" invention—a camera mount that was nothing more than a long pole carried by two movie sherpas, but that gave a swooping, careening look to shots . . . once the sherpas started running with it. But Sam also told them something else, something even more critical to their development as artists: before returning to his native Detroit, Sam told them his savvy blueprint for creating a limited partnership as a means of raising money for an independent movie.

Now here they were, many tax-sheltered investors and several years later, editing the result: *Blood Simple*.

The boys were excited to see me, of course—when they saw that I had come by automobile. They pounced on my old Honda like a couple of car-stripping hoodlums upon a Rolls in the Bronx, tossing my stuff haphazardly into their apartment. It seemed they needed one more piece of film to complete the complex puzzle they had crafted in *Blood Simple*. It was a critical storytelling image, a shot that would firmly anchor the movie's initial dramatic car scene between Frances McDormand and John Getz. Without it, none of the Jesse Vint aficionados watching the movie in their Chevy pickups under the Mississippi stars would have any idea what the hell was going on—rendering the scene, not to mention the remainder of the movie, so much completely senseless gibberish for them, thereby altering forever the course of—I mean, if you think about it and consider everything that would happen and all—American cinema history itself.

It was a moving shot of rain pelting asphalt at night.

And that is how I found myself cramped in the backseat of my

Joel and Ethan with cinematographer Barry Sonnenfeld during the filming *Raising Arizona*.

onda in the middle of a black and moonless night, riding the back-
untry roads of New York State, Ethan beside me, soaking wet and
ivering like an abandoned puppy, lanky Joel folded behind the
eering wheel, driving, and then cinematographer (today, *Addams
mily, Get Shorty,* and *Men in Black* director) Barry Sonnenfeld next
Joel, dressed in a rainproof poncho, pinching together a faulty
ble release connected to a huge 35mm movie camera mounted,
a rope and two-by-fours, to the Honda's front bumper, in search
a thunderstorm—any thunderstorm.

The day had started early, with a wake-up call from Barry relay-
g a radio forecast for area rain by nightfall. It took the rest of the
y to empty my Honda of possessions, then drive around New York
find film stock and a 35mm movie camera to rent on short notice.
four in the afternoon, Ethan and Barry were affixing the camera
the front of the car. As they wrestled with rope and two-by-fours,
e rain began to pour, in that powerful, muscular, torrential way
at only summer rains do. Barry stood in his rain-proof poncho,
han in nothing more than a T-shirt and jeans. Joel and I stood in
nearby doorway to shield ourselves from the rain and watched.
el smoked cigarettes, now and then calling out helpful sugges-
ns. "Hey, Eeth? Why don't you tie the rope around . . . yeah," he
uld say.

And also in that way that only summer rains do, the very instant
e four of us scrambled into the Honda, the downpour stopped. We
d not see rain again until around ten that night—the same
oment that Barry discovered the faulty cable release.

And so we drove on. Into the night, into the unlit hills of New
rk, far from the city lights. Who knew where we were? Time itself
emed to stop. After a few hours, it was as though we weren't even
iving on roads anymore—but floating along in the spaceship that
y Honda had become through a starless, measureless night. At one
int, the topic of Barry's daily nerve-racked, performance-anxiety
miting ritual on the set of *Blood Simple* was discussed at some
1gth. Years later I would wonder if his nausea was part of the rea-
n Joel and Ethan had been drawn to choose Barry as their cine-
atographer; perhaps it was something he had put on his résumé.

On the set of *Miller's Crossing*.

While it had been a fascinating evening of behind-the-scenes filmmaking excitement for me, it wasn't until around three in the morning that I realized the true scope of the Coens' patience, tenacity, inventiveness, and commitment.

From out of the nocturnal rural abyss, an all-night diner appeared, gleaming with colorful neon. "Maybe we should pull in there and think about this," Barry suggested.

"I wouldn't mind a cup of coffee," Ethan said, trembling.

"Yeah, coffee sounds good," Joel said resignedly.

He pulled into the diner's parking lot and shut off the engine. We sat quietly for a moment. "Hey, you know, maybe we should ask if they've heard of any thunderstorms in the area," Joel said.

Everyone perked up at this.

"Yeah," Ethan said.

"Yeah, that's a really good idea," Barry said.

Reinvigorated, they scrambled from the car and schlepped animatedly toward the diner lights.

Inside, the waitress poured coffee. "Have you, uh, heard any information about any thunderstorms in the area and where they might be located?" Barry asked.

We all looked up at her and waited expectantly. She shook her head at us and sneered. "No," she said, as if we were idiots or something, and walked away.

We all looked down at our respective coffees in silence. Ethan mustered one brief nasal exhalation that rippled his coffee like a breeze over a placid lake. Then all was silent again.

My God, I remember thinking. The boys are going to be famous.

Five years would pass before such an intimate peek into the Coens' creative process would come my way again.

It was the fall of 1987. Behind them was the modest success of *Raising Arizona,* a wacky, fast-paced comedy that marked the beginning of the boys' interest in kidnapping schemes as a plot device. Now Joel and Ethan were grunting and gasping with an untitled script they were writing about gangsters in a corrupt American town in the early 1930s. The script served as a kind of homage to Dashiell Hammett (if rifling through an individual's effects and taking what one wants can be deemed an homage), with a story that was part *Red Harvest,* part *The Glass Key,* but utterly quirky and Coenesque in tone. Though Joel and Ethan eventually titled the script *Miller's Crossing,* in those days they referred to it as *The Bighead,* which was their affectionate nickname for the main character, Tom, a pensive, tight-lipped antihero trying to cerebrate his way through the chaos of a gang war.

At first the boys were merely stymied by *The Bighead*—something about its plot being too complicated for them to figure out, they said. Before long, however, they would look wistfully back at their halcyon stymied days as they came face to face with a huge case of writer's block. The Coens tried various techniques to break through their block. They tried different writing locations. Come to think of it, that was their only technique.

Which is how they came to visit me. They stayed a week, and during that time, we mostly sat around drinking coffee, listening to Clancy Brothers records, watching *Jeopardy* every day at four o'clock, and eating doughnuts.

Finally, one night, we took a break from our grueling routine and went to see the movie *Baby Boom*. Soon after that, I started to notice an improvement in the boys' attitude. They attacked their doughnuts with greater appetite. Ethan seemed particularly taken with the *Baby Boom* theme song and began to hum it—incessantly, I thought. By the week's end, though there was no visible progress made on *The Bighead*, the elevation in the Coens' mood was palpable. They left beaming and thanking me profusely and saying how it had all been tremendously helpful.

Three weeks later, Joel and Ethan called me from New York to tell me they'd written a script called *Barton Fink*.

When I read *Barton Fink*, I saw immediately that the Coens had dealt with their problem in an ingenious way. They had taken their writer's block and made an effigy of it, an effigy named Barton—a rag-stuffed, immolated dummy vaguely resembling themselves, to which they could then also play the screaming mob that paraded it rebelliously through the streets while chanting simple but catchy slogans intended to humiliate. With a joyful shake of the pole they could make the flaming effigy dance and twirl in a comic mimicry of nightmarish agony. They could make Barton sweat in his underwear, give blood to a ravenous mosquito, and stare at the walls of his room with lip-sucking, blank-minded insentience until the paper literally peeled away. They'd force Barton to have his mind fucked and his foot kissed by blustery studio moguls, and make him open his bedside Bible to find his own writing contained in the Book of Genesis. They'd show him Hell. What connection any of this had to *Baby Boom*, I had no idea.

In the past, when thinking of the Coen brothers as filmmakers, I've always thought of sentimental incidents such as the above. I think of them, and of the many nitwit philosophical discussions I've had with the Coens during the creation of their movies. On *Raisin Arizona*, it was the critical difference between wacky and zan ("zany" is "wacky" with funny noises added); on *Miller's Crossing* the shameful paucity of "big dopes" in the modern stable of film actors (they blamed the system). I've thought of their eye for detail, in everything from the autographed picture of Barry Goldwater in Nathan Arizona's work office to the viscosity of the "goopus" oozing from the wallpaper in Barton Fink's sweltering hotel room.

When I was first presented with the idea of writing a book on Joel and Ethan's filmmaking craft by focusing on selected scenes as they evolved from script to storyboard to film, I was intrigued. I'd never really thought about it. Their movies had to get made somehow, I supposed. There had to be some sort of method, perhaps an interesting one. For something, certainly, distinguishes their public filmography from their early Super 8's. As Ed Coen, the boys' wry progenitor, will tell you anytime you ask, and sometimes when you don't, Joel and Ethan's early efforts offered no indication whatever that the Coen boys would amount to much in the world of cinema.

And yet now, despite the quirkiness and, at times, the inscrutability of their humor, despite the chaotically designed universe their movies portray, Joel and Ethan Coen are known throughout the movie industry as consummate professionals with a meticulous sense of planning, a confidence of vision from page to screen, and a vacuum-packed, if not anal-retentive, sense of quality control, tempered with practicality. The most commonly expressed opinion about the Coens by members of their production crew is the lack of confusion, the unchaotic, egoless, calming atmosphere that consistently pervades the sets of their movies.

The Coens, as it turns out, take their craft seriously.

And their craft is what this book is about. Before you jump in, however, let me make a few comments on interview technique as relates to this book.

In order to obtain something that vaguely resembled a formal interview with the Coens—something that, if not substantive, was at least without their usual word jazz of monosyllables and demi-sentences, their halting advances into non-sequitur and abrupt retreats into coma—it was necessary to separate them. At first, the technique felt nothing short of cruel, as the isolated Coen being queried would utter a half sentence, then look around curiously (Joel) or in panic (Ethan) when no one interrupted him to complete his thought. However, both soon warmed to their strange, new, brotherless environments, and before long were yammering away like a couple of retired B-Western directors in front of an audience of fawning film-school co-eds.

The interviews were conducted on the last day of shooting—driving to, and then from, the *Lebowski* set in Pear Blossom, California, where the production's final shot was, ironically, the movie's first: a lone tumbleweed rolling up a scrubby incline at night. Ethan was interviewed going *to* the set, in the late afternoon, with a third party driving. Joel was interviewed returning *from* it, in the wee hours of the following day.

So here it is, a book about the making of their seventh movie, *The Big Lebowski*.

Chapter 1

The Idea

The Homework in a Baggie

he Big Lebowski is arguably the Coens' most intellectually rambunctious script to date, not so much because it's brainy or challenging, but because, over the course of its short, 119-page life, it manages to romp through ore diversely arrayed, iconographic American pop cultural references than a Time-Life Books staff writer having a manic episode.

The script to *The Big Lebowski* opens with a cowboy chorus, à la ns of the Pioneers, crooning the classic range song "Tumbling mbleweeds" as a quintessential specimen of that plant group rolls a scrubby nocturnal incline and the Western-accented voice of m Elliott introduces the movie with a lot of quaint prairie jargon m Elliott is evoked by name in the script). The tumbleweed climbs up and over the hill's crest and suddenly we see the smoggy twilit expanse of Los Angeles yawning below us. As we follow our rolling vegetation's progress past various urban settings—a taco stand, a freeway overpass, a Pacific Ocean beach—and Sam Elliott's voice jaws nonsensically on, it quickly becomes apparent that we are not in a Western genre movie at all, but in Los Angeles in the early 1990s to follow the story of one Jeff "Dude" Lebowski, a bearded, long-haired, middle-aged '60s burn-out with no visible means of support, who smokes doobies, drinks White Russians, and has but one interest in life: bowling.

As the story begins, hooligans who have broken into the Dude's bungalow jump him and, with shouted threats and comments about "his wife" Bunny and someone named Jackie Treehorn, they aggressively demand "the money." They stuff the Dude's head in a toilet and urinate contemptuously on his rug. Then it hits them. The Jeff Lebowski they're after is supposed to be a millionaire. This guy looks like a . . . *loser.* And they depart, irritated at the inconvenience the Dude has caused them.

At his next bowling team practice, the Dude discusses the traumatic attack and rug befoulment with his teammate and best friend Walter Sobchak, a middle-aged, hotheaded gun enthusiast and Vietnam vet with a goatee, flat top, and tinted glasses, who is forever finding ways to work the subject of Vietnam bitterly into conversations. Moved by the Dude's lamentations that his urine-stained rug "really tied the room together," Walter, bellowing angrily as his wont, encourages the Dude to hunt down the millionaire whose name is also Jeff Lebowski and seek recompense.

Following what is but the first of many such lightly considered loudly presented suggestions from his teammate, the Dude seeks out the richer, bigger, wheelchair-beseated Lebowski, only to find himself quickly embroiled in a confoundingly populated, red-herring-infested, and mayhaps sham mystery that can be solved only by reaching deep into the Big Lebowski's dirty laundry hamper and pulling out . . . *Los Angeles.*

There's Bunny, the Big Lebowski's young trophy wife and star the porn flick *Logjammin'.* Maude, the Big Lebowski's femin cum-fluxus-art-movement painter daughter who rides naked in a suspended harness propelled by two attendants named Pedro and Elfranco while dribbling paint onto a horizontal canvas. Uli, Kieffer, and Franz, the black-leather-clad, motorcycle-riding, cricket-bat-swinging, lingonberry-pancakes-loving, would-be johnson-cutting former members of the late '70s Teutonic techno-pop group Autobahn and self-avowed nihilists. There's Jackie Treehorn, suave beach-party host and porno tycoon. There's the coffee-mug-hurling Malibu police chief and the mysterious fat guy in the VW bug. There's the severed toe with the emerald-green nail polish. And, of course, there's the attack marmot.

And that doesn't even begin to touch on the Dude's own highly complex inner life, which, during the course of the script, gives rise to two musical dream sequences, one of which features a magic carpet ride and Bob Dylan music, the other Busby Berkeley–style chorines, a Valkyrie, Saddam Hussein, and early Kenny Rogers music. Both feature an examination of such themes as sex, bowling, and . . . well . . . actually, that's about it.

Yes, the sprawling breadth of influences and references in *The Big Lebowski* renders it nothing less than a pop cultural potpourri, if not

Julianne Moore as a Valkyrie in the Busby Berkeley dream sequence.

an out-and-out hodgepodge. And yet, if it *is* a hodgepodge, it is one not without some sense to it, inasmuch as the metropolis of Los Angeles is exactly that—a hodgepodge. With some sense to it.

For, in the end, it is L.A. itself—or rather, the *idea* of L.A.—that the Coen brothers are after this time out.

"Jesus, I can't believe I'm stuck behind this guy!" Joel says, jerking out into the oncoming lane for a look, then quickly back again as a semi roars past us in the darkness. He sighs, then says reflectively: "You know, it's funny. There are more elements that are actually true in *The Big Lebowski* than there were in *Fargo*."

I brace my arm against the dash, elbow locked, and try to smile, affecting relaxed interest, as the speedometer creeps past 80. "Huh!" I say, but it comes out like a stomach punch.

The late-afternoon sun catches the copper tones of Ethan's scrubby beard. "*Fargo*, which was allegedly based on real events," he says, "in truth contains mostly made-up stuff. Whereas *The Big Lebowski*, which purports to be fiction, actually is based on real people and events." I nod, listening to the highway's gentle hum.

With *The Big Lebowski*, the fraternal filmmakers complete the trilogy of hard-boiled literary grave-robbing they began so long ago. Just as *Blood Simple*'s plot (despite its Dashiell Hammett–cribbed title) was fashioned in the style of an adultery-and-murder-happy James M. Cain novel, and the thoroughly Hammettian *Miller's Crossing*'s was the Coen's tribute to Pinkerton's man on Parnassus and his self-loathing heroes, so *The Big Lebowski* represents the brothers' special take on the third in the great triumvirate of American hard-boiled fiction writers: Raymond Chandler.

Exactly how the Coen boys arrived at Chandler's gravesite though—ostentatiously honking into their hankies, dabbing at their eyes, and clutching cheap flower bouquets as they surreptitiously eyed the corpse's jewelry—requires some telling.

———

It begins with a ratty-ass little rug.

A ratty-ass little rug . . . and three special individuals who collided in the Coens' creative consciousness at around the same time, like a dropped order of "three pigs in a blanket" in the pancake restaurant of their mind.

"You know Pete Exline?" Ethan says. "We were over at Pete's house, which was, you know . . . kind of a dump. Uncle Pete was in a bad mood for some reason. He was feeling down. So, we complimented him on the place, and he told us about how proud he was of this ratty-ass little rug he had in the living room—"

"What kind of rug?" I ask.

"Ratty-ass little rug."

"Oh, yeah," I nod.

"—and how it 'tied the room together.' So we told him that we, too, thought that it 'tied the room together.' We just kept talking about how the rug 'tied the room together.' You know how you beat something to death."

"Uh-huh," I nod.

"Pete is a Vietnam vet," Ethan continues. "Very bitter. Whenever the subject of Vietnam comes up, he says, 'Well, we were winning when *I* left.'" Ethan hyperventilates once through his nostrils. "You know, after the Gulf War was over in a hundred hours, or whatever the fuck it was, Uncle Pete called up and said, 'Look, it's a lot different fighting in the desert and fighting in canopy jungle.' Defensive acrimony."

Uncle Pete, the Philosopher King of Hollywood, also regaled the Coens with the wacky misadventures of his friend Walter. "At least think his name is Walter," says Ethan. "He's also a vet, who's sort of knocked around the movie business." One of the best Tales of the Friend of Pete's Whose Name Might've Been Walter involved a car that was stolen by teenage joyriders, one of whom inadvertently left behind his graded school homework. Homework that bore the joyrider's address. "So Pete and [the guy whose name might've been] Walter tracked down the kid and confronted him," Ethan says. Here, Ethan utters the one detail that congealed the story in s and Joel's mutual creative mind and led them to immortalize it

in a scene from *The Big Lebowski:*

"They had the homework in a baggie."

And so, *The Big Lebowski* as a script *inkling* was starting to take shape. The Coens had character fragments. They had a story event. They had a solitary line of dialogue. And with the rug, well . . . I suppose they had part of the set decoration.

But they needed more.

Enter John Milius, beret-and-battle-fatigue-wearing director of *Red Dawn* and *Conan the Barbarian*. "We met John Milius when we were in L.A. making *Barton Fink*," recalls Ethan. "He's a really funny guy, a really good storyteller. He was never actually in the military, although he wears a lot of military paraphernalia. He's a gun enthusiast and survivalist type. Whenever we saw him, he'd invite us out to his house to look at his guns—although we never took him up on it."

Aspects of Exline and Milius came together in the Coens' brains and began to merge, then mutate in a delightful way. And yet, there was still something missing.

That's when, conceptually speaking, a human being named Jeff Dowd wandered into the Coens' shared consciousness and made himself comfortable, as he has always done in the real world. The Coens had met him on one of their first trips to L.A.

"Jeff calls himself the Pope of Dope," says Ethan with his usual mixture of admiration and bemusement. "He is also called the Dude. He was a member of the Seattle Seven during the Vietnam years, and did time in jail for conspiracy to destroy federal property."

Today a producer's rep who still bears strong vestiges of his youth, Jeff "the Dude" Dowd, or rather his ideated self, brought the whole *Big Lebowski* script *notion*—for a *notion* it was rapidly becoming—a certain style, a certain ease of locution and hygienic sensibility, a certain special . . . *chemistry* that interacted pleasingly with the mutating aspects of Exline and Milius. The Dude!—a former '60s radical and pot-smoking burnout as a companion piece to a gun-loving, blowhard Vietnam vet!

Hell!—it could even be *his* ratty-ass rug!

And so it was that from three actual men, two fictional ones were born. And with them, *The Big Lebowski* script *idea*.

Explains Ethan: "You sort of know these people and hear these stories and they all sort of figure together in nebulous ways. The character of Jeff Lebowski, the Dude, is personally more like Jeff Dowd and Jeff's whole way of seeing things. And, not that the character is based on him in any literal way, but John Milius is sort of like Walter Sobchak. Pete Exline is a bit of both.

"One of the early ingredients came in setting these two characters beside each other—the Dude and Walter—and those two characters somehow seeming promising together," Ethan continues. "That, and the whole contemporary L.A. setting. Those two characters in conjunction with that setting seemed promising."

Says Joel: "The idea of setting it in L.A. started early because the people who inspired the story were in L.A."

Says Ethan: "You wouldn't see them in New York. I mean, you would, but they'd be different in New York. And since it was L.A. and it was a crime story, the whole Chandler thing started to figure in."

"Waitaminute," I say. "At the point we're talking about in the script's development, what crime thing did you have?"

"Well—the homework in the baggie," Ethan says.

Says Joel: "I remember when Pete told us the story about th
homework in the baggie and then later, in talking to Ethan about i
thinking that there was something quintessentially L.A. about i
but L.A. in a very Chandlerian way."

And that is what led the Coen boys to Raymond Chandler
grave: homework in a baggie.

In Raymond Chandler's wryly atmospheric, seedily romantic mys
teries, the city of Los Angeles is an oft-described character in i
own right, as Philip Marlowe, Chandler's melancholic white-knigh
detective, gallops to the far corners of L.A.'s lively terrain, exposin
himself to the wealthy and fringe-dwelling alike.

Chandler novels are usually two preexisting Chandler short sto
ries whose plots have been married (Chandler himself eschewe
matrimonial metaphors and instead described the process as "car
nibalizing"), featuring a detective who, over the course of the nov
els, becomes increasingly desultory and depressed to such a degre
that the mysteries frequently come looking for him, rather tha
vice versa.

The end product of all these Chandlerian characteristics is:
hodgepodge. For Chandler's novels are not so much exercises i
deductive reasoning as episodic page-turners brimming with quirk
characters and events, not all of whom or which necessarily ha
anything to do with the through-line story at hand, except tha
they embody the overall culture of L.A. with a deadly accurate an
searingly trenchant *je ne sais quoi*.

And searingly trenchant *je ne sais quoi* is a Coen brothers mair
stay.

For modern filmmakers, adapting Chandler to film has prove
problematic, since his vision of L.A. is so rooted in the '30s, '40
and early '50s. Updating Chandler demands from the filmmaker
whole new vision of L.A. that is consistent with Chandler, but tha
also believably embraces the present.

The most successful of the updated Chandler flicks is the 197

Robert Altman movie *The Long Goodbye,* scripted by Leigh Brackett. To Chandler's tough, romantic vision of L.A., Altman and Brackett added a development new to the L.A. landscape since Chandler's passing, but one that was thoroughly consistent with his world: the flake. In *The Long Goodbye,* hard-boiled wit is replaced by hard-boiled *nit*wit. Terse patter becomes rambling inanities. And the melancholic Marlowe becomes the easygoing Elliott Gould.

The Big Lebowski picks up where Altman's *The Long Goodbye* left off, with a flake-populated Chandlerian L.A. glutted with the wildly rebounding pop-cultural icons of the post-McLuhan universe.

However, says Joel: "[Altman's] *The Long Goodbye,* which our movie owes a lot to, is specifically Chandler, whereas *The Big Lebowski* is just kind of informed by Chandler around the edges. Our movie is not a detective story, really. It is only in terms of the kind of flavor you want to extract from it."

The Big Lebowski merely uses Chandler as a template: like Chandler's *The Big Sleep, The Big Lebowski* has a reclusive tycoon in a wheelchair with whom the hero must take an audience. Like *The Big Sleep, The Big Lebowski* has two women associated with the tycoon, one of whom is wild and sexually promiscuous with pornography in her past, the other older, more serious, yet sexually drawn to the hero. Like *The Big Sleep, The Big Lebowski* has a wealthy, corrupt playboy figure. But unlike *The Big Sleep, The Big Lebowski* has a hero who is not a jaded private detective in search of truth but an unemployed, pot-smoking doofus in search of a rug unsullied by urine.

Here a question must be raised.

"So, where the fuck does the bowling come in?" I ask.

"Uncle Pete belongs to a softball league," says Ethan. "He told us how he'd go and play softball every Saturday with Tony Danza and stuff. It just seemed funny. He'd describe the ambience—how they'd get into arguments and shit. It just seemed funny, Uncle Pete arguing with Tony Danza about whether he was safe at third or not.

"But, softball," Ethan shrugs. "I mean, who wants to look at that? The bowling—it's something to look at, with the whole Brunswick style. But also, it's a decidedly male sport, which is right, because *The Big Lebowski*, which we wrote around the same time as *Barton Fink*, is, like *Barton Fink*, kind of a weird buddy movie."

"And the Sam Elliott voice-over?" I ask.

Ethan shrugs, "We always like those devices—narration, voice-over. Also it's a Marlowe thing, since all the Chandler novels are told in his first-person narration. But it would be too corny just to have the Dude narrating, you know? There's something clearly wrong about having him do a voice-over."

Not to mention tedious, since Dude Lebowski's speaking style is vague, space-cadety, and incessantly profane. Still—why a Western-accented narration? Or why, for that matter, the crooning cowpoke chorus and the tumbleweed? Where the hell did those things come from? And suddenly I am treading an old battle-ground, asking a Coen to explain his meaning.

"The Western theme's just another thing that has nothing to do with anything but just seemed right next to the other things," says Ethan. Then he stares at me, as one might who was satisfied with what he had just said.

"Huh?" I say.

"We can supply stuff in retrospect," he continues, "I mean, in terms of what was right to us about the Western theme, but that might not be what in fact seemed right at the time. I'm saying my speculation about why we liked it wouldn't be any more interesting or valid than anybody else's speculation."

Okay, then. Well, since you asked . . .

In an effort to provoke Ethan into speculation, I wax pompous. I see *The Big Lebowski*'s opening, I tell him, and indeed the Sam Elliott voice-over that runs throughout the movie, as an arch statement on America's great Westward Expansion, with Los Angeles being the farthest geographic point in that expansion, not to mention the weirdest and most decadent. And insofar as this is a buddy movie concerning itself with issues of sex and manhood, I continue, the arch statement is really about the chauvinism of Westward Expansion, and, indeed, the absurdity of the pioneering American

Joel and Ethan with William Forsythe during the filming of *Raising Arizona*.

masculine mystique itself. But more than that, it's about the past, and the irony of a land professing a doctrine of newness and expansion that is in reality a vestige of its cowboy past.

"Yeah," says Ethan.

"Yeah?" I say, excitedly. And I didn't even have to go into my tumbleweed-as-bowling-ball and Dude-as-tumbleweed analysis.

"Yeah. I mean . . . yeah, probably," Ethan says. "It's not just that there's some connection between the West and L.A. It's that it's kind of wrong in a way, but also kind of right in a way. I mean, even the things that don't go together should seem to clash in an interesting way—like, you know, a Cheech and Chong movie, but with bowling.

"You sort of do it by feel and not with reasons," Ethan concludes.

And once again, I am left with the thought: Christ, do they really not think about this stuff?

Could it be that the Coen Aesthetic Process really has nothing to do with devising secret intellectual messages to torment viewers for their lack of education, but merely with grabbing images and themes and character types from wherever they may, and putting them next to each other, with the only provision being that these elements must either dovetail or clash in an interesting way?

I think of their approach to art in terms of some hands-on psychology test given to head-banging, deeply troubled children: *Joel and Ethan, I want you to sort these toys into groups that you think go together and then I want you to tell me why. Do that for Dr. Ludwig, will you?*

Do they really not think about this stuff?

Then I remember a story Joel and Ethan once told me about casting the characters of the bovoid escaped-convict brothers Gayle and Evelle Snopes in *Raising Arizona*. In explaining why they'd given the roles to John Goodman and William Forsythe, they simply said that those two fine actors were the only ones who, when placed next to each other in the room, caused the boys to spontaneously burst out laughing.

Joel and Ethan, can you tell Dr. Ludwig why you put those two fat men together?

There is undoubtably a very real disassociation the Coens have toward their art, as though the script, once created, is a separate entity, a third party, a thoroughly autonomous organism which they and anyone else can come and stand around, point at, and make observations about.

And while one can make good sport at the oddballishness of such pointed, ego-distancing behavior from a purely psychopathological perspective, still, from a purely technical perspective, it just may be a behavior that is critical to the Coens' success as filmmakers.

But let's get back to the process.

Let us, as Walter says philosophically throughout *The Big Lebowski*'s script, go bowling.

Chapter 2

The Script

Sleeping and Severed Toes

"What is the writing process like for you guys?" I ask Joel.

"Well, you know," he shrugs. "We sleep a lot."

"Yeah?"

"Yeah, we waste a lot of time. *You* know—you've seen us. We just kind of stare at the ceiling." He hyperventilates through his nostrils. "Actually, though, you know what's really funny, just between you and me and not for the book?"

"What?" I say.

"Trish and Fran [Ethan's and Joel's spouses, respectively], they're both always saying, 'I know you guys just go to the office and take naps.'" Joel's laughter implodes asthmatically. "It's true—it's actually really true. We deny it, but it's true." His laughter fades. "But I wouldn't want that in the book."

"Yeah," I nod.

"There's a lot of . . . you know . . . these things take a long time to ripen because—"

"There's a lot of cogitation?" I interject.

"Well, and a lot of procrastination. If it was all cogitation, it would go a lot faster," Joel says.

"Cogitation is not as dynamic a process as people make it out to be," I offer.

"I wouldn't know," Joel declines.

"Do you guys create outlines?" I ask Ethan.

"No," Ethan says. "It's all sort of really vaporous ideas and then we just start writing at the beginning. And that's how we crystallize the ideas—not by doing an outline, but by starting to actually write the scenes in order."

"Does one of you sit at the computer while the other paces?" I ask.

"Yeah," Ethan says. "We take turns. Although I usually type because I type faster."

"Do you ever take advantage of being at the keyboard and start to write something that you haven't been discussing, then have Joel look at it and see your take on it?"

"Yeah," Ethan says. "And sometimes the reverse. But it's not like one person will write an entire scene and present it to the other person. You might present one little idea or the beginnings of an idea."

"So neither of you writes on his own, then shows it to the other later," I say.

"Right. The other person is always there."

"Do you write your scripts in order, or will you write out of sequence?" I ask.

"In script order," Ethan says. "Sometimes, although not in the case of *The Big Lebowski,* we'll have an idea of something that might happen further down the line. But that's as close to outlining as we get. For instance, in *Barton Fink,* we knew we wanted to have Judy Davis's character, Audrey, turning up dead in bed with Barton. And we sort of steered the script into that idea. But, again, it was really vaporous until we got there."

"So when you know what's going to happen, you don't write that scene?"

"No. We don't actually write anything until it's in the script itself." Ethan reflects for a moment. "You know, at a certain point, especially in a movie like *The Big Lebowski,* you've got to think ahead. At a certain point, we had to sit down and say, 'All right. It's gotta be *some*body's fucking toe.' And that was before we actually got to the scene that discloses it, but well after the toe itself showed up."

"You had written in a severed toe, with no idea who it belonged to," I muse.

"Right."

"So is screenwriting something of a found process for you?" I ask.

"Yes. I mean, that's just an example, but that's the rule. We get the idea first—'Oh, it would be good if a severed toe shows up here—'"

"—But you don't logic it out in terms of some motivational need for the plot or character," I say.

"Yeah."

"You just come up with a bizarre image."

"Right. We want to goose it with a toe. And then you're left with the problem of whose toe it is."

"You're sort of deliberately setting up hurdles for yourself. Is that part of it, do you think?" I say.

"Well, yeah . . . I mean, that's a way to work, painting yourself into a corner and then having to perform whatever contortions to get yourself out," Ethan says.

"The ultimate example is *The Hudsucker Proxy,*" he continues, "in which we began the script with the idea of Tim Robbins's character jumping off a building. But then you're at the end of the script and you have to figure out how to save him. That stumped us for a while. And we had to resort to the ridiculous extreme of, you know, stopping time. That's the worse case. That's sort of the limiting case."

———

"Do you write thinking about camera angles and camera setups?" I ask Ethan.

"To varying degrees," he says. "Sometimes not at all. I mean, sometimes scenes are just conceived as 'This character says that and then this character says that.' While other scenes are like, you know, this one, obviously—the one we're about to shoot," he says, referring to the pointedly camera-conscious tumbleweed-climbing-over-the-scrubby-nocturnal-hill-into-the-L.A.-vista scene.

Which leads me to that most pointedly camera-conscious of scripted Coen scenes: the dream sequence, which is perhaps the most consistently recurring Coen cinematic storytelling device.

The Big Lebowski script has two dream sequences, and they're two of the most elaborate and ambitiously designed dream sequences yet in a Coen brothers movie. "So what's the fascination you guys have with dreams?" I ask.

Ethan shrugs. "It's just the cheap, gimmicky, obvious way to depict the character's inner life," he says.

"Uh-huh," I nod.

"But it's also very fun to do. Again, it's dovetailing things," he says, harking back to their technique of juxtaposing interesting but disparate elements. "You know, the character's a pothead. He's flying. The rug tying the room together. The whole flying carpet, *Thief of Baghdad* thing."

Ethan lifts his hand, drops it limply.

He shrugs.

I say to Joel: "The recent advances in digital computerized special effects technology have enabled you to do more of these fantasy type scenes, haven't they?"

"Oh, yeah. Absolutely," Joel says.

"Does that enter your mind when you sit down to write a script?" I ask.

"I don't know if it does consciously," Joel says. "But I mean, you sort of know in the back of your mind that something's po ble, that probably frees you up to—" He thinks about this, then shrugs off the thought: "You know, generally, we just blithely write what we want to see and then hope that there's some way of actually doing it without necessarily understanding how or even if it's possible.

"With *Hudsucker*," he continues, "which we wrote in the early to mid 1980s, before we'd even written *Raising Arizona*, there were a lot of things we put in it that would have been very difficult to do back then. So, it's become progressively easier and cheaper to use computers to do those things, and it's a great thing, but I don't know how much it actually affects you at the writing stage."

Around the time a script is completed, the Coens will start making phone calls to check on the availability of various parties key to turning their script into a movie. In the case of *The Big Lebowski*, Joel and Ethan's first call was to John Goodman, for whom they had specifically conceived and written the role of Walter. As it happened, their production schedule and Goodman's hiatus from his duties on the hit TV sitcom *Roseanne* did not mesh. Nor did it mesh with that of Jeff Bridges, for whom the lead role of the Dude was not specifically created, but whose casting, once the role was written and thought about, seemed predestined. And so *The Big Lebowski* was set aside and *Fargo* was written and made instead.

Suffice it to say there came a time when schedules did mesh, and the Coens flipped deeper into their figurative Rolodex, moving beyond the section figuratively labeled "Essential Cast" into the one about which this book is most concerned—the one figuratively labeled "Essential Crew." And *The Big Lebowski* was, as the Hollywood jargonists say, green-lighted.

At this stage in the process, many things happen, more or less, at once, as the Coens put together a production office, begin casting, and assemble a creative team. For *The Big Lebowski*, that team was the same one they had assembled for *Fargo:* Rick Heinrichs as production designer, Roger Deakins as cinematographer, and Mary Zophres as costume designer.

But, first and foremost, in the earliest dawning hours of this production stage of their process, Ethan draws many tiny stick ures in panels not much bigger than, say, a thumbnail, Joel m a list, and then both Coens sit down with a force of nature na J. Todd Anderson.

Chapter 3

The Storyboards

J. Todd Anderson, Force of Nature

S toryboarding is to filmmaking what tucking the inflated pigskin securely under your arm before you run for the goal is to the inflated-pigskin-carrying sport of your choice. Which is to say it's so fundamental a oncept to the process it seems too elemental, if not plainly idiotic, ꞈ mention—and yet it is frequently the reason behind the down- ꞈll or success of many a seasoned pro.

Storyboards are the drawn, sequential record of a movie's tended shots. They show how those intended shots will be ꞈmed, what camera movements, if any, will be used, and, gener- ꞈy, how those shots, which together compose a scene, will flow. ꞈt dissimilar in appearance to comic art, the storyboards are a tool ꞈrough which the filmmaker communicates his or her cinematic

J. Todd Anderson with Tricia Cooke and Joel and Ethan's assistant Alan Schoolcraft.

vision to the budget-minded producerly types, to the equipment-gathering production crew, and, perhaps most critically, to the film-maker's own self.

"Storyboarding," says Joel, "has always been an important part of our figuring out how to do a movie."

Exactly how much of a movie a given director chooses to story board depends largely on the director. Some may storyboard very little of their movies, preferring to figure out actors' movement and camera position spontaneously on the set. The director of an action movie may storyboard only the action or special-effects heavy scenes. But for those directors whose films are imbued with a carefully crafted sense of framing and an idiosyncratically distinct visual style, storyboarding becomes a very involved process. Alfred Hitchcock, Akira Kurosawa—these were big-time storyboarders. And though I can't say for certain, judging him purely on the basis of his overall body of work, my guess is that *Plan 9 from Outer Space* and *Glen or Glenda?* director Ed Wood was not a big-time storyboarder.

Joel and Ethan Coen, however, are big-time storyboarders.

. . . *Big*-time.

In fact, the Coens storyboard every single shot in the ent

movie—a very rare practice indeed. For them, the comprehensive storyboarding of a script is more than just a stage of pre-production; it is a philosophical point of view integral to their filmmaking process.

"So why *do* you storyboard the whole movie?" I ask.

Joel shrugs in that way a Coen does when he feels deeply about something: "The only way to make a decent movie for no money is to be very, very prepared, and to be able to answer very specific questions about what you need to see and what you don't need to see—and therefore, what you need to spend money on and what you don't need to spend money on. If the designer says, 'Do you want to see this wall and this wall?' it's a lot easier to give him an answer if you've worked out exactly how you're going to shoot it. Then they spend money on two walls instead of four walls.

"We learned the habit early on, when we were making movies for nothing. And while it's true that storyboarding the whole movie isn't a very common practice even among people who make low-budget movies, for people who *do* make low-budget movies it's a *very* good idea, I think." He shrugs. "We started doing it because, temperamentally, we were insecure. We're not necessarily good extemporizers and we particularly prefer not to extemporize camera coverage on the set on the day we're going to shoot. It's just not the way we like to do it.

Says Ethan: "I think a more obvious question would be 'Why don't other people do it?' You storyboard everything because you want to think about how you're going to shoot the movie before you actually shoot it. I mean, it seems self-evident."

"Why don't other people do it?" I ask Joel.

"They probably think it's, you know, stifling and throttles down any spontaneity. They probably think it's stodgy." He laughs. "I have no fucking idea."

"But you guys storyboard *everything*," I say to Ethan, "even the parts where people are just sitting across a desk talking to each other."

"That's for everybody else in the production, so they can know what has to be prepared. They can look at it and say, 'Oh, it's just that obvious goddamn scene where we have to supply a desk. We don't need the crane that day.'"

"Which saves money?" I ask.

"Well, it helps you to work efficiently. We think in terms of time—working quickly, efficiently. The norm is to carry everything in terms of lenses, cranes, whatever, just in case a director decides, 'I want to do this today.' So, yes, it saves money in that respect. If you carry everything through the whole goddamn shoot, and the art department prepares every direction because, who knows, they might want to look at it every which way—that's more expensive."

Says Joel: "As we've made more movies, we tend to do it somewhat less for more straightforward kinds of dramatic scenes."

Says Ethan: "The whole completeness thing—it's really not because we're fetishistic about storyboarding everything. It's just so people can confirm the obvious: it looks like a scene with two people talking and it *is* a scene with two people talking. The reason you have to confirm the obvious is that sometimes you don't do the obvious. You might have more elaborate ideas for coverage."

To some extent, the Coen brothers have never fully shed their low budget, independent filmmaking skins, and their approach to storyboarding reflects the survival instinct of that special breed. There exists a kind of unexamined logic that says the lower the movie cost, the easier it will be to get a movie made; and the more you control your budget from the outset, the better tolerated your artistic eccentricity will be.

But it's also important to note that—aside from the comprehensiveness of their approach—storyboarding, for the Coens, may not be the same experience it is for others. Because they don't merely storyboard the entire movie, they do it with a uniquely individual storyboard artist from Dayton, Ohio, named J. Todd Anderson—affable, creative, salt-of-the-earth sort with whom they have worked since *Raising Arizona*.

Says Joel: "J. Todd understands quickly what it is we're trying to do.

Says Ethan: "J. Todd's quick to get it. He understands what ba coverage is, so you can describe the banal things to him quickly and spend more time on the nonbanal things, which are harder to describe and more interesting to talk about."

"Explain the J. Todd Experience for me," I ask Ethan.

"While we're with J. Todd, Joel's got a shot list in front of him and I've got my thumbnails in front of me," Ethan says.

"And you describe what you want?" I ask.

"It's not just describing what we want. It's sort of rethinking it as we're talking about it," Ethan says.

"So it's a collaborative process?" I say.

"Yes. To varying degrees. Sometimes it *is* just laying shit on him and other times not. It has to do with J. Todd's personality and, you know, no doubt ours. J. Todd will never suggest something like 'Wouldn't it be better from over here.' It's not like that. He's somebody who thinks completely visually, so when we're talking and thinking it out, he's the ideal sounding board."

"Will J. Todd ever suggest a shot?" I ask.

"His personality is such that he would never presume to do that, although he does influence the shots tremendously without trying to," answers Ethan. "This whole sort of thinking-out-loud thing— you just try to put across what you're thinking about to somebody. You just sit around chatting about it and all of that sort of ends up figuring in."

"It starts stimulating J. Todd and—"

"—stimulating us," Ethan says. "It's a weird feedback thing."

"But he himself would never suggest a shot?" I say.

"No," Ethan answers. "Although he might well stimulate one."

Says Joel: "J. Todd's a good catalyst. He also has a great eye of his own. He's a real aesthete in his own way, and in a strange way he has a lot of input into our movies. We talk to J. Todd about things that don't necessarily have to do with the storyboards. He's got an interesting point of view on design issues, how things should look. What a costume should be like or what a person's posture should be. We've often discussed with J. Todd how posture is everything. How a character carries himself physically. It's an important thing and it's something that often gets expressed in the storyboards. And

Joel's shot list

1. Close on the Dude in the tub smoking a joint
2. DUDE's POV—thru the open bathroom door—the cricket bat smashes the answering machine
3. Close on the Dude's toes sticking out of the water at the far end of the tub
4. Wide on the nihilists entering the bathroom—Dude's POV
5. Med. Close on the marmot at the end of his lead
6. Full on the bathtub as Dieter throws the marmot in
7. Reverse for marmot in and out—also hold for POV thrashing with marmot-on-a-stick
8. Pop in closer on the tub for thrashing with the marmot
9. LOW^ ground level CLOSE on the marmot for skittering and sneezing
10. LOW^ 3-shot of the nihilists next to the tub—Uli leans into a leering CLOSE SHOT for "I say vee cut off your chonson!"
11. WIDE Dude's POV of the nihilist's backs as they leave
12. Med. Close on the Dude as his head is pushed back in the water
13. INSERT—Close on the tape recorder being smashed by the cricket bat

Ethan's thumbnail sketches

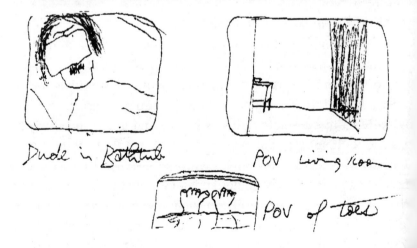

Dude in Bathtub

POV Living room

POV of toes

58

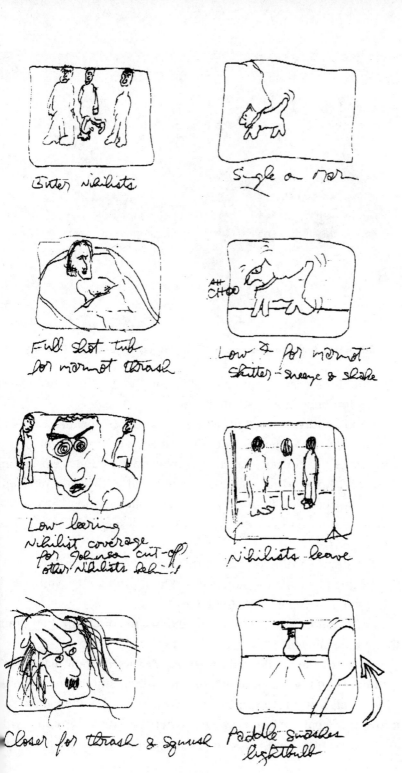

Enter nihilists

Single on man

Full shot tub
for marmot thrash

Low 3 for marmot
Skitter - sneeze & shake

Low leering
nihilist coverage
for Johnson cut-off
other nihilists behind

nihilists leave

Closer for thrash & squeal

Paddle smashes
lightbulb

Ethan and Joel lining up shot with cinematographer Roger Deakins.

it's something that he understands a lot about. You know? Most people don't give it a lot of attention.

"J. Todd notices a lot of things about clothing," Joel muses. "And he's one of the only people you'll ever meet who can tell you pretty much every American manufacturer of tractors and farm equipment and know what colors are associated with those different manufacturers, you know? That's what I mean when I say he's a real aesthete. He has a very interesting, very specific point of view on design issues.

"The storyboarding process with J. Todd is more than just a storyboarding process," Joel concludes. "I don't think most storyboard artists get as involved as J. Todd does."

Says J. Todd: "I just try to be the extension cord from their brain to my little clipboard." A frightening notion indeed.

But his comments regarding *The Big Lebowski* recapitulate Joel' comments on the free-roaming nature of their storyboard sessions "There's all sorts of stuff that can be done with a bowling alley. Yo know, those balls are moving everywhere and those pins are flyin all over the place and the kinetic energy and the style is just over whelming. The culture that's behind it, too, is another thing that I think attracted them immediately, because it's so American. We talked and I said, 'Yeah, that's gonna be cool.' We would talk a lot about the ball chucking up in the ball-return, and then it hits the other balls. All that kinetic energy there that you can cut away to. And the polished wood floors—they're beautiful—we'd discuss all that. The way bowling alleys are set up with little kids running and playing in the back, and then the Brunswick styling—they got me excited talking about that Brunswick styling. You know, it's so cool—the ball returns look like F-86 Sabre Fighters. It's not just bowling, it's style."

Each of the Coens' movies, says J. Todd, has its own visual tone—a personality, if you will—that allows the movie to walk and talk on its own. "It's like a Beatles song. It has its own character," J. Todd explains. "But Joel and Ethan don't say, 'This is the character of the film, not this.' Instead, they tell me little things. And then I respond and they say, 'No.' Now and then, I'll finally get along their line of thinking. And then I start to understand the tone of their film. But I don't try to anticipate what they're gonna do.

"In a script, it could say, 'Guy runs down the street.' Ordinarily, you'd automatically assume that you're gonna track with that guy. Well, not so fast—Joel and Ethan have a different idea. This guy's not only gonna run down the street, they're maybe gonna cross over him sideways. You know, 'No, we're not gonna track him laterally, what we're doin' is we're flying over the top of him and then coming down behind him.' Or maybe they're gonna be on a mountaintop and you see this little dot runnin' down the street."

At the outset of a storyboarding session, J. Todd draws a floor plan of the scene. The Coens show him where in the floor plan the camera will be for a given shot, and J. Todd transposes it in his head. Then they adjust for angle. For the non–film school matriculator, J. Todd explains: "There's an axis line on every camera, and the actor's nose is gonna tell you where that axis line—their eye line—is gonna work. And I track that."

He goes on: "So, I'll hold the clipboard up there and I'll draw. I'll say, 'From this angle?' and they'll say, 'Yyyyyyyeah . . . ,' and I'll

FLASHBACK   VENICE HOUSE

side & rear
houses

Ring
doorbell

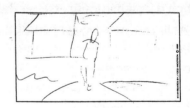

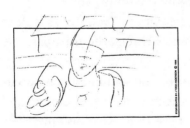

OTS

draw the head size and they'll say, 'Bigger, bigger, bigger—stop,' and then I'll draw a little cross on his face and I say, 'Which way is he looking?' And they'll say, 'Yeah, his eye line's there,' and then we track the longitude of the axis angle, which is vertical, and all of a sudden we've got ourselves a composition that we're working with, and I throw that down and move on to the next shot.

"They pretty much have a good idea within twenty or thirty degrees what they want," he continues. "Though, over time, I've noticed that they see shots from opposite directions. Ethan will see it running from left to right and Joel will see it running from right to left."

"Huh," I say.

When the storyboard process is going like gangbusters, says J. Todd, the ideas are pouring out of Joel and Ethan, and J. Todd is pencil-drawing as quickly as is humanly possible. And—if you believe the man—the Coens occasionally shout at him with all the Beat euphoria of two Allen Ginsbergs standing over a frenzied, *On the Road*-typing Jack Kerouac. The "lightning sketches" that J. Todd produces are almost abstract in their brevity and spareness. As soon as a shot's basic concept is captured, he slaps it facedown, unnumbered, and moves on. If the sketch is wrong, he X's it, drops it to the floor, and tries again. Typically, he has three types of pages bearing one, two, or three empty frames or panels. The Coens call them one-bangers, two-bangers, and three-bangers.

"If it's a pretty standard setup, then we'll use one frame," says J. Todd. "But if it's a—say, for instance, the guy walks from the door to his desk, I'll use two panels. But if the guy's gonna drive a car through a cornfield and take out a couple of telephone poles and then run over a small child, that's usually three or four panels."

"Huh," I say.

"Or maybe six panels," he continues, "and I go into triple panels and we just keep drawin' till the shot ends."

Later, when the dust has settled, J. Todd goes back through his abstract lightning-sketched one-, two-, and three-bangers and draws in detail—first in pencil, then, over that, with pen and ink.

Often, if the cinematographer has joined the production at this point, he will sit in on the storyboarding sessions with J. Todd and the Coens to offer his own input. J. Todd feels strongly about the importance of the cinematographer's contribution to the story-boarding process. With every production, he asks that they share an office so that the storyboards-in-progress will always be available to the cinematographer.

Despite the labor-intensiveness of storyboarding the entire movie, the process between the Coens and J. Todd Anderson takes only about six weeks. This is partly because of J. Todd's own mani-acal speed, but also because the Coens don't let the actual locations chosen for a scene shape the storyboarding. The opposite is more commonly the case in a movie production, lengthening consider-ably the storyboarding phase. "Joel and Ethan make up stuff and then the locations fit the storyboard," says J. Todd. "In *Raising Arizona*, they said, 'We don't do research. What we do here dictates the location.'"It is a feat achievable only through a precise sense of shot framing.

In the end, when the Coens' movie is edited in post-production, says J. Todd, it cuts together pretty much the way they story-boarded it. "The screen direction, the tone, the pacing—it's all pretty much been discussed in the storyboard," he says. "When I first saw *Raising Arizona*, I was just absolutely overwhelmed by the fact that I recognized every shot in that movie."

"So if J. Todd started with you guys on *Raising Arizona*, who did you use for storyboarding on *Blood Simple*?" I ask Ethan.

"Three local people in Austin," recalls Ethan. "It was weird. One guy would do storyboards. Another guy would do floor plans. And a woman was there who seemed a sort of secretarial help. We'd sit there with three people. It was odd."

"What was odd about it?"

"It was very quiet," Ethan says.

"So, you had no chemistry with these people? Is that what you're trying to say?"

"Yeah," Ethan says. "I mean, they were perfectly nice. But, you know, you'd sit there and describe the shot and—"

"—everybody would stare at you?" I suggest.

"Yeah," Ethan says, eyes brimming with horror at the memory. "Pencils poised. They treated us like royals. And the storyboards— they looked like drawings from *Highlights for Children*. Like Goofus and Gallant. The people in the drawings were very—"

"—stiff," I say.

"—*square* and stiff," Ethan says, his troubled eyes gazing off into the distance.

"Tell me about your first experience storyboarding with J. Todd," I say.

Recalls Ethan: "It was less quiet than the Goofus and Gallant sessions on *Blood Simple*." Then he adds chipperly: "Although, as I said, they were very nice people."

"What do you like about J. Todd's style of storyboarding?" I say.

"They're really amusing to look at, especially when he knows who the actors are," Ethan says. "They've got more going on. I mean, they're not Goofus and Gallant panels. More like Mort Drucker panels," he says, referring to the famed *MAD Magazine* cartoonist. Ethan muses.

Then he says, proudly, "As a matter of fact, he's getting more and more like Mort Drucker."

The Coens' storyboard meetings with J. Todd are different from other pre-production meetings, says Joel, in that storyboarding starts out with a very specific agenda—the shot list—and then turns into a general discussion about the movie, whereas the other meetings start out as general discussions, then grow specific. But they all share one common trait. Both Coens describe, indeed, emphasize, them as being more in the nature of "discussions" than meetings.

In fact, "discuss" is quite possibly the word most frequently bandied by Joel and Ethan when they speak of pre-production. It's an important distinction to them, this difference between a "discussion" and a "meeting," and not just because they're uncomfortable with their success and trying desperately to avoid looking like white-shoe managers of a cinematic sweat shop.

It's because the Coen boys are actually serious about this whole "rethinking" business. It's how they get things straight in their heads. They discuss them. Over and over again.

"It's like doing successive drafts on a piece of writing." Ethan says. "Each time you improve it. You think more about how you're going to cover the movie. Like rewriting, it's not just an exercise in penmanship or typing—it's an exercise in rethinking everything."

For the Coen brothers, each step along the path leading up to a movie's production is an opportunity to discuss and reassess their perspective on the project. An opportunity to open their mouths and say things to the external world, then listen to hear what comes back. Or, to put it metaphorically:

The Coens' heads are marsh, and spoken words are the tidal ebb and flow that allows the marsh to cleanse the sea. Over and over.

Over and over again.

Can simple chat really be part of the Coens' process? Is conversational give-and-take really that self-conscious an act for them?

Yeah.

And yet, as we shall see, there lurks a paradox.

Chapter 4

The Human Coendition

A Discussion on Hiring Technique

The paradox is this: while the Coens rely on repeated discussions with essential crew in order to help them rethink their script and fine-tune their vision of it, Joel and Ethan, by nature, are not what you'd call "gabby types," and to that end, one of the things they do when building their production team, as best I can tell, is to select people with whom they communicate well so that they don't have to talk much.

In my interviews with Roger Deakins (cinematographer), Rick Heinrichs (production designer), and Mary Zophres (costume designer), uniformly I was told that the best thing about working with the Coens was how they really knew what they wanted and how well they communicated what they wanted to their crew. Knowing the boys for as long as I have, I could only stare at my interview subjects in slack-jawed amazement. "And . . . how exactly do they communicate it to you?" I'd ask.

Invariably the answer was a reflective brow-knit, and, after a moment's pause: "Well, for one thing, they storyboard the whole movie."

Right! My point exactly! This whole thing, this whole "process" business based on "thinking things out" and "communicating" through the script and the storyboards, is nothing more than an elaborate ruse to avoid having to talk!

"So, when you communicate with your crew," I ask Ethan slyly, "what sort of form does it take? They read the script and you meet with them and—what, do they give you a presentation of their ideas or do you give them a presentation of your ideas? How does it work?"

"It's just a conversation. We bat ideas back and forth," Ethan says. "We discuss things."

"At length?"

"Well, it's not like we instruct them that we want A, B, C, D, E. It's more on the order of saying 'Yes, this seems right,' or 'No, that doesn't seem right.' That's more how it gets nailed *down* than through any sort of initial conceptual discussion."

"And yet, your movies have such a strong and idiosyncratic vision. How do you instill an understanding of that vision in your crew?" I say.

"It doesn't have to do with vision," Ethan answers. "That make it sound like a personal thing. It's a very *im*personal thing. I mean you've written this script," he continues. "You like to think it ha some sort of life. And if it does, then everybody's interest is in serving the story and the discussion is about what's appropriate for th story or the character."

"So then, your communication comes through the script—fro the fact that people have read your script and that they've inferre the movie's tone from the writing itself?" I say.

"Yes. A big part of what makes it easy to work with Rick, a

with Roger to an even larger degree, is that a lot is unspoken. They have a rapport with the material. They read the script and they get it, so a lot of the basic conceptual stuff is never discussed, because it doesn't have to be.

"I mean, some people, however much you talk, you sort of can't get it across. Or on a personal level you can't connect. So it's like a taste thing: you gravitate toward people who have similar styles and tastes. Either similar or complementary. I mean, I'm not sure if Roger's and Rick's tastes in movies are much like mine or not. Actually, probably they aren't, I don't really know. What's important is they get it. They're very sensitive. They can feel their way through it, kind of like we can, you know what I mean? You wouldn't believe how much we *don't* talk about with Roger."

"I'd believe it," I say.

"But I'm saying that's a remarkable thing," Ethan says. "We could work with somebody else and talk volumes and nothing would work."

"But *would* you talk volumes?" I ask. "I mean *really*?"

"Sure," Ethan shrugs. "Actually, some actors like talking a lot. I actually find that interesting sometimes. Some people like it and some people don't and either is fine. And it's not just actors," he says, suddenly feeling generous. "I mean, whoever—Roger, Rick, Mary . . ."

"Okay, then tell me who likes to talk at great length who's not an actor?" I challenge him.

"Well, J. Todd, for example."

I frown and fall quiet.

"—And Roger is sort of the other end of the scale, and Rick's somewhere in between. Mary is also somewhere in the middle and not either extreme."

"So, if I may summate," I say, "you're telling me that what you and Joel look for in a production crew is an immediate, intuitive grasp of the material, of the script and the kind of movie that script should be—"

"Yyyyyes—" Ethan says.

"—but you're not looking for clones," I quickly add. "You're merely looking for people to whom the script is a meeting ground. They may like to talk a lot or not. But the thing you share in common with them is the material, not a common vision of the world, personally speaking."

"Rrrright," Ethan says. "That's exactly right. Not of the world in general or movies in general or whatever."

On a roll, I continue in a booming voice: "And whether they may talk a lot or not doesn't really matter to you, because the fact that they have an intuitive understanding of the material in the first place means you don't have to communicate anything to them, because they already know it!"

Ethan stares at me as one might at someone who was annoying.

And so we find that communication—and even talk itself as a method of talk avoidance—must be included as key to the Coen brothers' filmmaking process.

And while one—say, me, for example—might feel like a moron saying it, it is undeniable that, if nothing else, the Coen brothers are consistent: through the thoughtful pre-selection of talented, imaginative, intuitive people, the Coens are, in a sense, storyboarding their human resources.

So. Let's go meet the crew.

Chapter 5

The Cinematography

Orange Night

*I*n our look at the creative production crew triumvirate, we begin at the non-gabby end of the Coen Standardized Verbosity Spectrum, with cinematographer—and J. Todd Anderson officemate—Roger Deakins.

Roger Deakins grew up in the seaside resort town of Torquay in southwest England. A painter before he turned to photojournalism and then film, Roger attended the National Film School in London, afterward embarking on a career as a documentary filmmaker. Roger's documentary work led him to war zones and even around the world in a boat. In the mid-1980s, he made the transition to feature films as cinematographer on *Il Postino* director Mike Radford's *Another Time, Another Place* and *1984*. Throughout the second half of the '80s, Roger quickly developed a reputation for powerfully evocative, versatile camera work—proving himself equally adept at the gritty, the surreal, and the romantic—on small, intelligent, mostly British films such as *Sid and Nancy*, *The Kitchen Toto*, and *Stormy Monday*.

Says Roger: "Some cinematographers like just to create a visual style and the script's maybe not that important to them. I didn't get into film just to create images. I like to work on films that I would also like to have directed."

Then came *Air America*, a comedy about the CIA's early involvement in Vietnam, starring Mel Gibson and Robert Downey, Jr. It was big. It was American. It was . . .

" . . . a bad experience," says Roger, "in the sense that it ended up being a buddy-action movie rather than the film that I and a lot of people expected it to be, which was a dry, ironic, political satire. It was a big film and the filming of it was like being in a war zone itself. We had nineteen cameras working at one time. It was the kind of filmmaking where you're so distanced from any sort of personality, all you're really trying to do is get through it."

Returning from Thailand after his tour of duty with *Air America*, Roger reflected on his future in film. "I said, 'Well, that doesn't work for me,'" he recalls. "'I don't really like that kind of filmmaking. I'll move out of London and live in the countryside where it's less expensive. I'll just do small, personal films.'"

Then his agent told him about another American script he'd been sent. It was called *Barton Fink*, and was written by the Coen brothers.

"She advised against it," Roger remembers. "She said, 'I don't think you'll like it. It's really bizarre. It's not for you.' I said, 'You must be joking! Send it to me, for God's sake! I'd die to work with them!'" Appends Roger in that wistful way only a Britisher can: "And so I met them in Notting Hill Gate in London."

He continues: "The funny thing was, they asked Roger Spottiswoode, the director of *Air America*, what I was like, and he said [unenthusiastically], 'Oh, you know, he likes to shoot with one camera. He likes to use prime lenses.' And it was everything tha

Roger Deakins.

Joel and Ethan like to do, of course, but nothing Roger [Spottiswoode] likes to do. Roger likes to shoot with lots of cameras and zoom lenses. He really covers it with a huge amount of shots and makes the film in the editing room, whereas Joel and Ethan shoot very tightly. And that's what I like doing."

For those not up on their cinematographic-ese, the "prime lens" of which Roger speaks is any fixed focal length rather than a zoom lens. Says Roger, "It means you're locked into shooting at 50mm or 32mm or whatever the lens's focal length is, whereas with a zoom lens you can change the focal length during the shot. Which I think is a little bit of a sloppy way of shooting—pulling back on the lens as opposed to moving the camera. Using fixed lenses creates a sort of precision to your work. It forces you to think."

Think. That word again.

Needless to say, things went rather well when the Coens met with Roger in London. Roger went on to become the Coens' cinematographer on *Barton Fink, The Hudsucker Proxy,* and *Fargo,* the last of which earned him his second Oscar nomination (his first being for *The Shawshank Redemption* the previous year).

———

Listening to Roger cerebrate about his craft, one immediately understands why the Coens chose him as their cinematographer. For example: Roger likes to prelight his sets as much as possible. "There is nothing more expensive than keeping a whole shooting crew waiting," says Roger. "It's better to spend that rigging time with a smaller group of electricians and, when you come to the shoot day, have as little holdup as possible.

"I like to operate the camera as well," adds Roger, "and because I'm doing that and talking to Joel and Ethan, it's important to spend as little lighting time on the set as possible. That way I can concentrate on other things."

"Why do you like to be the camera operator?" I ask him.

"I don't know, maybe it's from doing stills and documentaries," he says. "I just like to be involved. I like to be involved with the actors. I like to have that one-on-one relationship with the director.

"Cinematography is more than just the way the picture's lit," he says. "The framing and the move of the camera are so much of it. And it's often the camera operator's relationship with the director that leads to the way the shots are blocked. The times that I've used operators, I've sat in dailies and found myself craning my head, trying to get the screen to move left or right. If I do it myself, I've only got myself to blame."

But in addition to that, says Roger, since he prefers to light through the camera, being his own camera operator allows him to make quicker adjustments in lighting if needed, and to signal more easily any minor changes he might want in camera tracking movements to the dolly grip. In short, says Roger, it provides him both flexibility and control.

In the beginning, as is the case with almost everyone who works with the Coen brothers for the first time, Roger was concerned about the logistics of working essentially with two directors. "I soon realized, though, that I could ask either of them if I had a question," says Roger. "It didn't matter who I turned to. It was whoever was free and nearest or most convenient. They were so totally in sync.

Over time, Roger found that the odd telepathy Joel and Ethan apparently shared between themselves was extending to him a

74

well. Or as Roger puts it: "After a while the trust comes. I mean, often now, I'll change a lens after a take and I won't go over to Joel and Ethan. I just do it, and if they don't like it, they'll say. But that happened just once on this shoot.

"It's better to work tight like that," he continues. "You work faster. And I think it's like the relationship I have with my crew: if I trust them and give them responsibility, then it's just a nicer thing. They feel a part of it more. And so it is all the way down the line."

"Joel and Ethan are very different from most film directors I've worked with," says Roger. "I haven't worked with anybody else who storyboards to their extent. In *Barton Fink*, I think there were probably only a dozen shots we did that weren't in the storyboards. Everything else you could match to the storyboard. That's unusual.

"Their scripts are very visual and very specific. Once you've read the script, you kind of know what you're in for," he says. "It's quite a lot easier to work with Joel and Ethan than other people; they come with such concrete ideas—and yet at the same time, they're not dogmatic."

But in what way exactly does the Coens' unique approach affect the average on-the-set working day of a cinematographer?

Well, for starters, there's blocking, says Roger.

"The majority of the directors' way of working is you go with the actors on the set in the morning, you rehearse, and then you block it," says Roger, adding that some directors will actually turn the scene over to the cinematographer to block completely. "They'll say that's the scene—okay," says Roger. "And I'll have to stand in the corner and write down the scene and do the shots.

"With Joel and Ethan, you don't do that, because it's basically been blocked for you. The blocking is in the storyboards.

"Now, of course, that changes on the set," he is quick to add, "because the actor might want to do something or Joel and Ethan might have another idea or I might have an idea of how to do something different or combine shots or whatever. But basically, at the beginning of the day, you've got a number of storyboards that you have to shoot on a particular day.

"There were a couple of scenes in *The Big Lebowski* that weren't quite storyboarded, because it was at a location they didn't have until late. So we basically blocked the scenes in the morning before the crew arrived and went through the shots, just walked around, looked at the scene a few times, worked out the angles that would work best, wrote them down, and shot it.

"That was kind of unusual for Joel and Ethan," Roger laughs. "But, I have to say, it was nice to see that they could do it that way as well."

And, of course, another area of the cinematographer's job description that feels the impact of the Coens' unique approach is that of camera coverage, an area where the director's neurotic inner self can be dynamically exposed for all to see, at its most nakedly and timorously insecure.

"Directors generally tend to shoot a lot of coverage to play it safe on a sequence," says Roger, "but Joel and Ethan sometimes will do just one shot of a big, big piece of acting. They'll say: 'Okay.' I'll say: 'You know, we should do another one.' 'Oh, you want another one?' 'Well, I mean, wouldn't it be nice?' And they'll shrug. 'Oh, okay. Let's do another one.'"

Roger laughs. "Whereas other directors might fret, 'Well, it might work, but what if it doesn't work? We need another cut here and let's do a close-up here and let's have a shot of him doing this!' Joel and Ethan know what they want. They've seen that they've got it and they move on. It's a confidence they have."

The Coens' initial pre-production meetings with Roger often address how real the look of a given movie should be, says Joel, or its level of stylization. "I think that's something you have to decide early on," says Joel. "It informs a lot of decisions about how a movie gets shot. How much you move the camera and how it's lit. How slick it is, how gritty it is, that sort of thing."

The Big Lebowski, being such a slaphappy grab bag of juxtaposed styles and imagery, just in its subject matter alone, was not an ea

Joel, first assistant director Jeff Rafner, William Preston Robertson, Ethan, John Turturro, and Roger, watching playback of the scene just shot.

look for the trio to pigeonhole, admits Joel: "With *Barton Fink,* we could talk specifically about how we wanted to stylize it and what exactly we meant with certain kinds of stylizations. And with *Fargo,* we talked about a more reality-based look and how we wanted to express that—which, actually, is just another way of stylizing something: insisting that it be real-looking.

"But *The Big Lebowski* is a weird mix," says Joel. "There are parts of the movie that want to be real and contemporary-feeling, and other things that are very stylized, like the dream scenes. And then there's the bowling stuff. So this is more of a mix, this one. And I think it's that mix that makes it different and interesting from the things we've done before."

Says Roger: "With *Fargo,* I remember we discussed wanting to make it more naturalistic, more observational, like a documentary, because of the whole idea of it being a true story. At one point we even said we should shoot it on longer lenses and the camera would be static and would observe from some point in the room. We never stuck to that discipline, of course. But because we'd had that whole discussion, I think the look of *Fargo* is different and it

77

does have a sort of slightly observational, quieter look to it than, say, *Hudsucker* or *Barton Fink*.

"I'm not sure I ever really had a handle on what *Lebowski* should look like," muses Roger. "It's such a mix, I don't think it has one style. It's not like *Fargo*—it's not observational. But it's not the heightened, stylized look of *Hudsucker*."

Roger's efforts were further complicated by the sheer stylistic breadth of the locations being used.

When he lights a scene, Roger prefers to use natural sources—another holdover, he suggests, from his documentary days. While he may choose to boost a source, Roger likes for a given light to have a plausible reason for its presence. When shooting on a constructed set, of course, this is accomplished easily, because the environment can be manipulated easily.

Location shooting, however, is another story. Locations usually cannot be manipulated easily and are much more limiting in the choices available. Thus, says Roger, compromise is an understood part of any location shoot. But with so many locations being used in *The Big Lebowski*, and of such pointedly varying style—from the Dude's tired Venice Beach bungalow to the opulently baroque Lebowski mansion, from Jackie Treehorn's swinging, jazzy glass-and-concrete Malibu pad to the retro fluorescence of the bowling alley and the theatricality of the Busby Berkeley dream sequence—finding a unifying visual tone was, in short, a challenge.

So how did Roger create a *Lebowski* look?

When he first read the script to *The Big Lebowski*, says Roger, his impression was that it was much darker than *Fargo*. Although it came nowhere near the level of *Fargo*'s violence, he says, he felt in certain ways *The Big Lebowski*'s characters were darker and its atmosphere seedier.

And so in keeping with that reaction, says Roger, "*The Big Lebowski*'s photography is more naturalistic and raw, and probably a lot more contrasty than *Fargo*. On the other hand, the camera moves are less observational than *Fargo*. The camera moves are more stylized, but the lighting and the look of it are more realistic and gritty."

Roger describes his work: "I mean, you've got these fantasy scenes which sort of pop out as being very crisp and monochromatic. They're very stylized, much crisper, and more highly lit to afford greater depth of focus. And with the [Dude's] beach cottage, it's kind of seedy and the light's pretty nasty. There's less fill light. It's less molded, and it makes the whole feel of the thing harsher and more gritty. To that end, I've shot most of the film on high-speed stock, which also adds a bit more grittiness to the overall image. I shot it on 5279, which is a 500 ASA stock."

Still, a visual bridge was needed that would connect the movie's disparate settings with their disparate tones. Roger's solution: the night.

The night.

Of course. The place the Dude is forever stumbling in and out of as he wanders through the grotesquely cast Chandlerian odyssey that is his life.

"Because there was so much night," says Roger, "I thought, well, I'll make use of that. And so I decided early on that I would give the night sequences on the street a special look. I'd do them really orange. The night light, instead of being the usual blue moonlight or blue streetlamp, would have a very orange, sodium-light effect.

"It was something I started to do on *Fargo*," he says, "but I thought with *The Big Lebowski*, I'd go much further. And so all the night exteriors are pretty orange, except for where the lab tried to print it out."

As the shoot progressed, Roger found that in the dailies—printed takes from the previous day's shooting—the lab was trying to "correct" the color of the orange night scenes.

"It's damn well going to go back in," he laughs.

There is one more fundamental, aesthetic bent that Roger shares with Joel and Ethan that we have not touched upon. It is a bent that, while not necessarily integral to the Coen Process, is a linchpin of what might be called the Coen Look. It is a bent that might lie at the very nexus of those who love Coen movies and those who do not.

It is their proclivity, if you follow my belly-flop into the next chapter, for—

Chapter 6

The Human Coendition, Part 2

Wide-Angle Lenses

That's right—*wide-angle lenses!*

Among those critics who it could never be said were big fans of the Coens' cinematic *oeuvre*, a commonly registered complaint is that, as filmmakers, the Coens are icy-hearted, with an emotionally sterile vision of the world that betrays contempt for their characters and their audiences. Setting aside the most obvious retort to such criticism—which is, of course, "You say that like it's a bad thing"—I, as an admirer of the Coens' work, have a long-treasured theory that a substantial part of the blame for the "cold and sterile" beef, if I may call it that, lies in the Coens' general choice of lenses, which tend to be wide-angle ones, which aesthetically, I think, has a distancing effect on the viewer.

With a wide-angle lens, the depth of focus in a picture frame is increased, allowing for more intricately designed compositions in which a host of things may be presented for the viewer's consideration simultaneously—but in so doing, a wide-angle lens elongates the world dimensionally, pulling forward the closest objects in a frame and pushing away the farthest. It exaggerates the distance between the various objects in a frame, emphasizing their detachment from each other. And at it's most extreme, it can cause a human subject in close-up to appear to have a nose some two feet in length, with eyes quite nearly located on the side of the head. I mean, to some, that could be a distancing thing, you know?

I fly my lens-width/movie-critic-alienation inverse ratio theory past Joel.

"It's something Roger kids us about," Joel says, genuinely considering the point. "It is true that we've favored wide-angle lenses in a lot of the things that we've done, the most extreme example being *Raising Arizona*. And *The Big Lebowski* is shot almost entirely on 28mm and 32mm lenses, which are fairly wide."

"What is it you like so much about them?" I ask.

"Well, wide-angle lenses do a number of things," Joel says. "For one thing, they make it easier to hold focus for a greater depth. And they make camera movements more dynamic. The longer the lens [long, in this sense, being the opposite of wide], the less you feel the camera moving. And with movement away from or toward the camera—that's also more dynamic with a wide-angle lens."

Joel muses. "Longer lenses, because of their shorter depth o' focus, tend to single things out more and isolate your attention on specific details more. But do wide-angle lenses really distance peo ple? I'm not sure that's true."

"Well, what about the sterility thing?" I prod. "You don't thin having a broader depth of focus, in which everything in sight sharply focused, might create a sterile feeling in certain instances?

"You know, I don't think that's true, either," Joel says. "I think has more to do with how you want to compose things, actually."

I latch onto this. "Well, then, what do you strive for in compos tion?" I ask.

"I'm trying to think of—see, I never think of it in the abstract li

Examples of shots with wide-angle lenses.

that," he says. "It's the same with the lens business. It's not like there's a conscious decision to use wide-angle lenses. You just put up different lenses and you go, 'Yeah, I think that's the way to go' or 'I want to see this.' It's not like you have a theory about how it should work. But I really don't think it's the lens."

"What do you think it is?" I ask.

"I think it's because they don't like our characters," he laughs.

"Yeah, but it's one thing to have unlikable characters as protagonists," I suggest, "and it's a whole other thing to go and distort their fucking faces."

"And so not only are our characters unsympathetic, they're ugly?" Joel laughs. He thinks about it. "Well, there's the whole glamour lens thing—you know, if you use a longer lens, it's more flattering to people. Instead of stretching out, it pushes it in." He shrugs. "You may be right. Who knows? It's an interesting theory."

He goes on, "See, though, what you could say is that a very styled approach with a camera in general will be off-putting to people, because they may feel it takes them out of the movie.

"I mean, that's distancing. If you have a lot of wacky angles or something. You know, like in *Raising Arizona*, where camera movement and camera angles are kind of baroque. But it's not just a function of the focal length of the lens itself. It's in how you move the camera and what kind of set-ups you're framing. I just think in the end, it's a combination of things as opposed to only the focal length."

Roger shares the Coens' affinity for wide-angle lenses, though if lenses were Marxism, Roger would be a Swedish socialist to the Coens' Peruvian Shining Path. Says Roger: "I see things wider than most directors I work with. But Joel and Ethan see them wider than me. I suppose that's why we get on, because I see things like that."

"Joel said that you kid them about their penchant for wide-angle lenses," I say.

"Oh, I did on *Barton Fink*," Roger answers. "When we were initially talking about *Barton Fink*, I think *Raising Arizona* was probably nearer to what they were thinking of. But I told them that I thought *Raising Arizona* was—well, I didn't like the wide-angle lenses moving at such high speed and tracking so fast. The distortion becomes so active. I don't really like that.

"And so on *Barton Fink*, we had this sort of joke. They'd be thinking 25 millimeters and I'd be thinking 28 millimeters [the lower the number, the wider the lens]. So sometimes I would start with a 32 on the camera and they would think, well, it should be 25. So we'd compromise and end up at 28 mil." Roger smiles. "The whole joke was, I was kind of weaning them onto longer lenses—though really still quite wide."

Roger recalls his weaning schedule: "On *Hudsucker* we used some very wide lenses—we used a 10 and stuff—but basically, the lens of choice for a wide shot was probably a 28 or even a 32. By the time we got to *Fargo*, the wide-shot lens was 35 or 32, though we did do some wide-angle there. But on *Lebowski*, I don't think we used lens wider than 28 or 32. And we've also been using some long lenses. For the Simi Valley road scene, we did a long-lens point of view with something like a 200 mil, which is unusual for them." Roger laughs. "But they said: 'That's cool. Long-lens point of view. Oh, okay.' They liked it."

To give a clearer perspective on how this tug-of-war for millim terage compares to the real world, Roger explains: "Most features, a close-up would be shown in 85 mil. We've never done that. We shoot our close-ups, you know, 40, or 50, if you're very close. Maybe a 65, if you're *really* tight. But I don't think we've ever shot an 85-mil close-up."

"So why do *you* like wide-angle lenses so much?" I ask him.

And here, Roger says a truly amazing thing: "I think they're more intimate."

HUH?!

"Oh, yeah," he says. "If you're five feet away from somebody on the 40-mil, shooting a close-up, I think it puts the audience closer to that person."

He goes on: "If you're across the room there on a long lens, the audience won't see this corner of the room. If you're closer on a wider lens, you've got the same size on the actor, but you've got a much wider frame on the background. You get a sense of the environment. I like that. I like to see a person in his space. I don't like just having a fuzzy background and being all close-up. Plus, long lenses reduce the perspective and flatten the frame. It's a stylistic thing. And I think that's why Joel and Ethan like them—they like putting the audience right there."

I am stunned by this diametrically opposite line of reasoning. I try, as the Dude might say, to get my head around it. "Well," I say. I nod. "Well, then . . ." I look up at Roger. "Well, what do you think accounts for the 'cold-hearted sterility' accusations?"

"They don't do over-the-shoulders," Roger says. "We did it in *Fargo*, because of the whole documentary, observational thing. When you shoot a documentary, you usually do over-the-shoulders, because you're sitting behind the person. If you look at Joel and Ethan's storyboards, always, if there's a two-sided conversation, the camera's in between those two people. Personally, I love over-the-shoulder." Roger sits back, reflects. "Maybe it comes from doing so many documentaries."

Roger's gaze drifts to a spot in space.

I examine the same spot, and mull.

Chapter 7

The Production Design

Brunswick, Fluxus, Googie, Noir
(Though Not Necessarily in That Order)

A rt departments are confusing—at least they always
have been to me. You go into the art department
offices of a given movie production, looking for the
person in charge, and you encounter a person iden-
tified to you as the art director and a person identified as the production designer. Now, let's say a fistfight breaks out between the
two. Then, suddenly, into the room bounds the set designer, with
the art department coordinator close behind. And both of them
jump the art director.

My question is this: are you witnessing an act of mutiny or an
abuse of power, and by whom?

"Production designers *used* to be called art directors back before

Gone with the Wind," explains Rick Heinrichs, *The Big Lebowski*'s production designer, and, as such, the buck-stopper of the art department. "Art directors have always been the head of the art department in the managerial sense. You manage the art department: you manage the workflow, you manage the construction department, and you keep things moving.

"Over time, though, production designers have come into being, as more of a director's pet, if you will, where you're actually allowed to be in your ivory tower and conceive. Of course, it doesn't really work out that way—there's still plenty of hands-on work. But primarily you conceive the film with the director and the art director.

"The best production designers," says Rick, "my favorite ones, are like Bo Welch, who came up through the art director ranks. That kind of production designer knows exactly what the art director job entails. And he facilitates better because he knows what needs to happen. In the creation of whatever flights of fancy, that kind of production designer is always keeping things in the realm of what is doable and realistic."

Did I mention that Rick also rose up through the art director ranks? And before that, through the ranks of some of the other art department brawlers in our hypothetical fracas.

After a remarkably peripatetic childhood spent in California, Minnesota, Massachusetts, Maryland, Tennessee, Illinois, New Hampshire, and Vermont, Rick, the son of academicians, attended college at Boston University of Fine Arts, where he studied sculpting. Deciding, after BU, that what he really wanted to do was animation and cartooning, he went to the Visual Arts Center in New York City, where he took classes from famed cartoonist Will Isner and others. From there he went to the Disney School at the California Institute of the Arts, and from there to employment at the Disney animation department, where he worked as an assistant animator, sculpting stop-action models.

It was while at Disney that Rick met, among other young and talented animators, Tim Burton, working with him on the class shorts *Vincent* and *Frankenweenie* as well as in the nascent development of *Tim Burton's The Nightmare Before Christmas*. Post-Disney

Rick Heinrichs.

Rick continued to work with Burton on *Pee-wee's Big Adventure, Beetlejuice* (where he first worked under production designer and aforementioned role model Bo Welch), *Edward Scissorhands,* and *Batman Returns,* as well as with others on *Ghostbusters II, Joe Versus the Volcano, Soap Dish,* and *Tall Tale: The Unbelievable Adventures of Pecos Bill*—all movies noted for their striking, stylized art direction. Through it all, Rick steadily rose up through the art department, from jack-of-all-trades and model builder, to visual effects director, to set designer, to assistant art director, to art director.

Rick's first job as a production designer came on the Showtime cable channel's *Fallen Angels,* a film-noir-inspired series that featured classic hard-boiled stories from the 1940s, filmed as shorts by such well-known directors as Steven Soderbergh (*sex, lies, and videotape*), Michael Lehmann (*Heathers*), Agnieszka Holland (*Europa, Europa*), and Peter Bogdanovich (*The Last Picture Show*). "It was a week-long shoot for each one of them, and it was one right after the other," says Rick, who describes the experience as "production designer boot camp."

Fallen Angels also provided Rick with something of a compressed career in budget filmmaking. Says Rick: "There were only a limited number of sets we could build, because we had a limited budget. We were constantly shifting things around, pretending we were making one five-hour movie, trying to figure how to reuse stuff and make it look different. While you're finishing up with one director's film, you're meeting with the director for the next week. And you may telephone the director two weeks down the road, and it was like boom, boom, boom, boom."

With his extensive experience working on so many fanciful, heavily stylized art-directed movies and the transferred credits from his recent crash course in noirish budget filmmaking, Rick Heinrichs was quite nearly pre-Coenized by the time he sat down with the boys to talk about what would be his first feature film production design job.

In his meeting with Joel and Ethan, Rick told them that the thing that impressed him most about the script they had titled *Fargo*, the thing that he was really looking forward to working on, was the dream sequence. "It had an Indian in it," Rick recalls fondly. "I remember the dream sequence was very shadowy and there were eagles and stuff like that. I loved it, and in the interview I went on and on about it. And finally, Ethan, I think it was, said, 'Yeah. You know . . . we're cutting that out, actually.'"

Rick Heinrich's office is a pop culture potpourri, if not an out-and out hodgepodge, all unto itself. Lying around on tables are model of the sets for the Busby Berkeley dream sequence: varyingly size black-and-white miniature dioramas of surreal, bowling-theme dreamscapes, complete with tiny figurines, looking like the grade school projects of a prepubescent Salvador Dalí, if he had grown u in, say, Cleveland.

Leaning against a wall in the corner are a pair of giant prop sci sors. Scattered across his desk and along a shelf behind him a books on film noir, including one called *The Detective in Hollywoc* books on the Fluxus art movement and on the 1980s, and nume

The Inca party.

ous books just generally concerning L.A. "A lot of bungalow court-yard books," says Rick.

Over on a bulletin board is thumbtacked a picture of the Jackie Treehorn house. Underneath it are cutout magazine pictures of late-'50s and early-'60s bachelor-pad-style furniture. There is also a young, velour-shirted, Brylcreemed Robert Goulet posing on an album cover and a similarly retro one of a young Tony Bennett.

And then there is Rick's sketch of Jackie Treehorn's Malibu beach party, depicting fire and night and men with tall, feathery head-dresses.

"Yeah, that came out of nowhere. They just one day said, 'Oh, by the way—the beach party is Inca-themed.' So we had to think, 'Well, what does Inca mean?' It was clear what they had in mind was a very Hollywood-looking party in which young, oiled-down, fairly aggressive men walk around with appetizers and drinks. So there's a very sacrificial quality to it."

oel and Ethan are unique not only in the fact that they write it, rect it, and produce it, but that they are so very visually attuned,"

Rick says. "To them, the look of a movie can be another character as well. For instance, in *Barton Fink* [for which Dennis Gassner was the production designer], when the wallpaper is peeling and falling down onto Barton—that's a visual idea. It's a sensibility that the set itself is a character. And *The Hudsucker Proxy* [again with Dennis Gassner] is the most thoroughly stylized and designed picture that they've done. The visual elements in that movie are just so integrally a part of it."

It is ironic, then, that, considering the Coens' and Rick's backgrounds in stylized cinema, *Fargo* would be their first collaboration together.

Recalls Rick: "I told them, 'I've been involved in a lot of very designed, stylized films, and to me *Fargo* seems like, not dry, but certainly very naturalistic.' And they said, 'Yes. We want to do something different this time.'"

But what Joel said about cinematography in the chapter before last is equally true for production design: *making something look real is just another way of stylizing it.*

"People ask me, 'So you designed *Fargo*? Well, like, what did you *do*?'" jokes Rick of the snowy, down-coated movie. "Some people think that that Paul Bunyan statue is really near Brainard. They go looking for it. And I feel good about that.

"It's not that you go somewhere and shoot it the way it is Minnesota doesn't look like *Fargo* at all," he says. "We carefully selected places, nudged things here or there with snow or neon—took reality, gave it a little kick.

"If you look at *Fargo*, even though they were going for a much more naturalistic look, the design is still very much a character. Whenever there were landscape shots of white snowfields blending into the sky and the horizon line was lost—anything that was in that field became like a graphic image on a piece of paper. Even just a fence going off into the horizon became like a pencil mark. And they turned a real parking lot into an almost Oriental design—you know, where it's straight down and he's walking to his car? It's just beautiful.

"That's something I love playing with in the more stylized stuff the push-and-pull between two-dimensional and three-dimensional. And actually, Roger Deakins is, I think, incredibly adept at composing the frame. I'm amazed by his compositions. He can really find ways to organize and balance elements beautifully.

"*Fargo*," concludes Rick, "was a really good lesson to me in appropriateness and holding back and saving elements." Or as Roger has said about lighting scenes, *a lot of lighting is about taking it away, not putting it on.*

It was a lesson that would serve Rick well for his next Coen brothers venture, *The Big Lebowski,* about which Joel and Ethan first told Rick at the *Fargo* wrap party.

"Usually by the time I see a script, it's the script we're going to shoot. Unless of course they cut out the dream with the Indian and the bird," says Rick.

"How do we communicate? There is a certain process of osmosis. It's a combination of having worked with them now for a couple of pictures, knowing their work very closely, and, of course, taking for granted that they *want* me to work with them because I have a somewhat similar take on things in a visual sense."

"When you meet with them for the first time, do they start talking or do you start talking?" I ask leadingly.

Answers Rick: "I feel like I'm supposed to start talking about what I think, so I do. And as I talk, some of it's right on and some of it's not right on. But it prompts their thoughts. And they answer with 'Yeah,' 'You know,' or 'Well . . .' Ethan does a lot of 'Well, you know . . .' They have a somewhat deadpan delivery. And once or twice I've been a little unsure whether they were being serious or not. They don't leave me hanging too long, twisting in the wind. I'm more used to it. I think I can tell now."

"With Rick," says Joel, "discussions usually get organized by location."

Reasserts Ethan: "It's not like we have a planned-out agenda or have conceptualized how everything in the movie will look down to the set dressing on each set. It's more a question of, when you're

A fedora-bedecked man stands in the shadows, staring out at the city lights. A match flares under his Lucky Strike. For a quick, chiaroscuric moment, we see his face: eyes haunted by recent murder, upper lip quivering with psychosexual conflict. He blows out the match. A backlit puff of smoke curls up from his silhouette—a not-too-subtle brimstonic portent of the damnation that is his fate, beckoning to him like a dark-eyed siren lounging in a cheap cocktail dress on the rocky shore of lust. The man turns up his collar. Touches the warm gun in his overcoat. And steps out to face the night, his bowling bag clutched firmly in his fist.

His bowling bag?

That's right. Because this isn't just any film noir. This is that sub-of sub-genres, the rarest of the rare, the hardest of the boiled: bowling noir. Or, as the French might say, *bowling noir.*

The arrival of *The Big Lebowski* marks a bold return to this long-forgotten genre, a return to those mean alleys down which a man

talking to Rick or whomever, being able to say, 'Yes, this seems right,' or 'No, that doesn't seem right.' A lot of it is discussed in terms of the negative case."

"The process of making things concrete," explains Joel, "is often just making it clear what you don't want to do."

Says Rick: "There are directors who may think that they have a visual concept of what they want to do, but they are not so visually attuned. With those directors, you could walk in with almost any idea and act real enthusiastic about it, whatever the idea is, and sell it to them. 'Now, you're going to love this!' And their reaction is going to be 'Whoa!' and 'Good!' and 'Yes!' and 'It works!' And that's why a lot of Hollywood movies look the way they do.

"But Joel and Ethan are always exercising their sense of what they want," continues Rick. "They're always asking, 'What do we need?' and 'What's more important?' and 'What's the priority?' They are always prioritizing. Because they really want to get to the essence of their film. That's what's so great about working with

must roll, a man who is not himself mean, a man who . . . what's that? You've never *heard* of bowling noir? Huh. What film school did you say you went to?

Let's start with basics. The term film noir has been greatly mis-used in recent years to describe pretty much any low-budget movie in which nudity, violence, and a smoke machine figure heavily. Among hard-core celluloid pinheads, however, true film noir is an American cinehistorical phenomenon that spanned the decades between 1940 and 1960. Generally, the '40s–'60s era in America was a time when the great suburban exodus from the city took place, when hard-boiled pulp novels were all the rage, when the post-total-war male power structure became terrified of the strength and independence American women had shown in the labor force during WWII, and when there were a number of expatriate Austro-Germanic directors kicking around Hollywood desperately seeking any outlet, however inappropriate, for their arty Teutonism.

Thus, film noirs were noteworthy for vertiginous angles and kinet-

(continued)

them. Anything you're working on, you know that they really need that thing, because they've decided that they don't need these other things."

And what sorts of things did the Coens discuss with Rick about *The Big Lebowski*?

Says Ethan: "In talking about *The Big Lebowski* with Rick and Spell [set dresser Chris Spellman], discussions were always framed with 'We don't want to hit this too hard.' No lava lamps or that kind of shit. No Day-Glo posters on the wall of his house. No Grateful Dead music on the soundtrack. And though I personally am a Cheech and Chong enthusiast, and would often attempt to pull Jeff Bridges's chain by telling him we were basically just making a Cheech and Chong movie—well . . . we didn't want it to look like a Cheech and Chong movie."

"So what did you want it to be?" I ask innocently.

ic camera usage, claustrophobic set designs, a theatrical use of light and shadow; for presentations of the city as "evil" and likewise strong, independent women. The noir actors were often as deadpan and terse as the cinematography was flamboyant. And the screenplays were classic tales of badly flawed, deeply obsessed individuals unable to escape their predetermined fates.

Right.

Now throw in some bowling—and you've got the idea.

For the uninitiated, a good bowling noir to start with is *Double Indemnity* (1944), the best and best-known of the genre. What makes *Double Indemnity* a bowling noir is the scene in which Fred MacMurray, quite nearly febrile with the realization that Barbara Stanwyck is seducing him into a plot to murder her husband, delivers the following jittery voice-over:

> . . . I knew I had hold of a red-hot poker and the time to drop it was before it burned my hand off. . . . I didn't want to go back to the office, so I dropped by a bowling alley at Third and Western and rolled a few lines. . . .

Ethan tries to explain their very specific, yet ultimately asymptotic intent: "We wanted things to be bright and poppy, because that's consistent with the whole '60s thing, and because there's a splatter artist in the movie. But the '60s thing in terms of 'psychedelia' was something we really wanted to avoid."

Rick offers his own example of the First Principle of Coen Physics: "Maude has a line of dialogue in her loft when she's talking to the Dude, about how men have a hard time saying the word 'vagina.' Now, in creating the art for her loft, we could have had a lot of vaginal artwork all over the place: gaping mouths, sculpted orifices, what-have-you. But that's just hitting it too squarely and it's not really that interesting anyway."

Rick continues: "From the beginning, Joel and Ethan said that Maude's character was based on artists in the Fluxus movement. So, naturally, I went and did research to find out what the heck Fluxus was. Well, it was a movement in the '60s which contended that art is a record of the creation process itself, rather than a stand

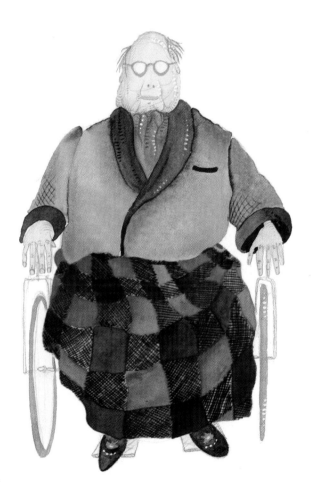

Big Lebowski

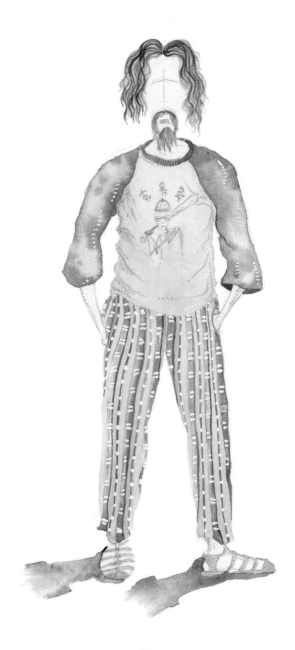

Dude

Quintana

Donny

Walter

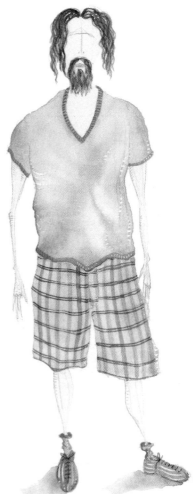

Dude

Corvette Owner

Dude

Walter

Maude

Chorine

The Great Room Scene

Lens: 32 mm

35 mm

Scene 16

32 mm

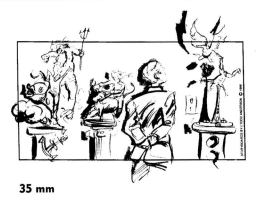 

35 mm

50 mm

Scene 16

32 mm

The Quintana Scene

50 mm
48 frames per second

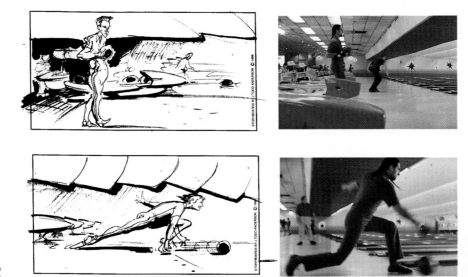

35 mm
96→24 fps

Scene 18

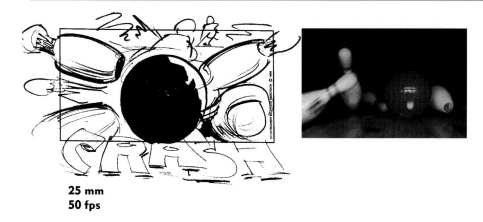

25 mm
50 fps

35 mm

28 mm
12→24 fps

Set-up 1. RAKING the houses on the block as Quintana enters in profile and rings the bell.

28 mm

Set-up 2. WIDE looking down the walk toward the street as Quintana approaches into CLOSE-UP – for scene.

32 mm

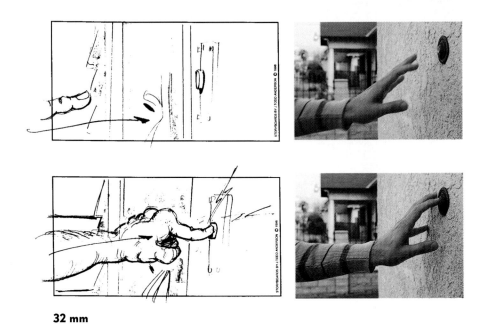

32 mm

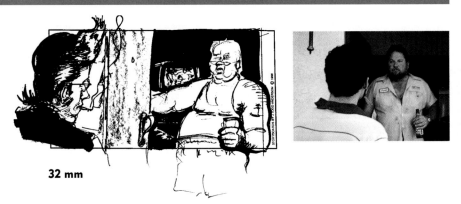

32 mm

28 mm

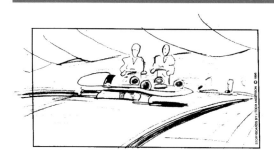 

65 mm

32 mm

Scene 20

The Corvette-Smashing Scene

Set-up 1. PULLING Walter – ¾ in front of him with the house in the background. **HINGE** to the Dude's car as Walter pops the trunk.

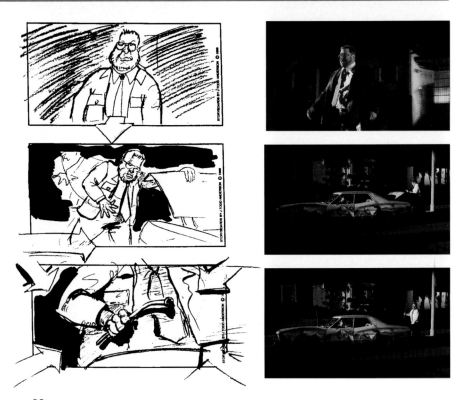

32 mm

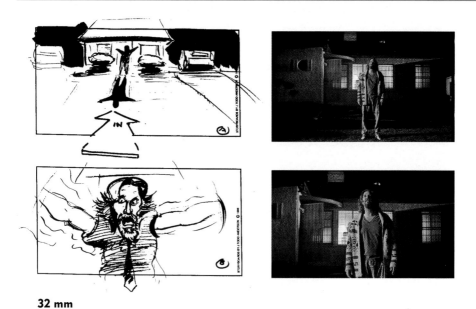

32 mm

25 mm

25 mm

25 mm

Scene 52

32 mm

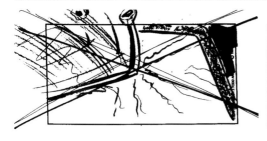 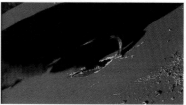

35 mm

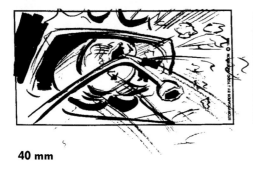 

40 mm

25 mm

32 mm

Set-up 11. CLOSE on Donny cringing.

32 mm

Set-up 12. MEDIUM on Walter as the enraged Mexican runs up behind him and grabs the crowbar on the backswing.

32 mm

Set-up 13. CLOSE on Walter puzzled, watching the enraged Mexican.

32 mm

Set-up 14. WIDE on the Dude's car as the enraged Mexican enters the foreground. PLAY through him whaling on the Dude's car.

32 mm

Set-up 15. CLOSE on the enraged Mexican whaling on the Dude's car.

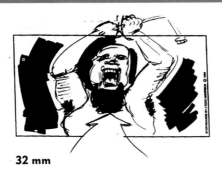 

32 mm

Set-up 16. CLOSE on child standing on the doorstep of the Mexican's house.

50 mm

Scene 52

Busby Berkeley Dream Sequence

32 mm

These three elements for shot were combined in computer.

28 mm

32 mm

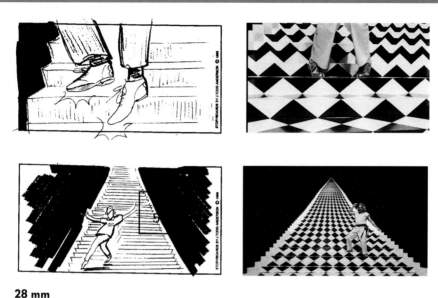

28 mm

18 mm

Set-up 6. LOW ANGLE 2-SHOT as the Dude, pressed up behind Maude, helps her with her release and follow-through.

28 mm

Set-up 7. LOW ANGLE looking down the lane as the chorines straddle the lane and the ball rolls between their legs.

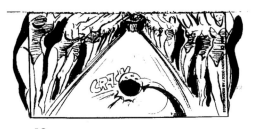 

18 mm

Set-up 8. PUSH IN TRACKING shot as the Dude, suspended over the lane, moves between the chorine's legs. He barrel-rolls onto his back.

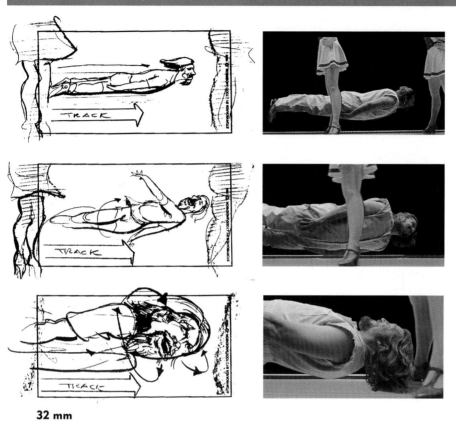

32 mm

Set-up 9. WIDE over the heads of the chorines as we move with the Dude down the lane.

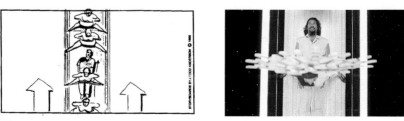

28 mm

Set-up 10. CLOSE on the Dude from overhead as he moves under the chorines' legs and looks up their skirts.

35 mm

Set-up 11. The Dude's POV looking through the chorines' legs at pins.

18 mm

Set-up 12. The Dude's POV of pins scattering.

 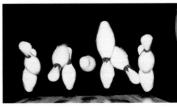

32 mm
60 fps

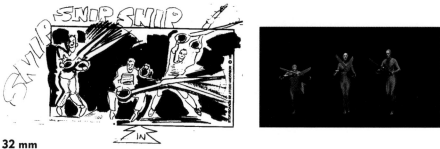

32 mm

These three elements for shot were combined in computer.

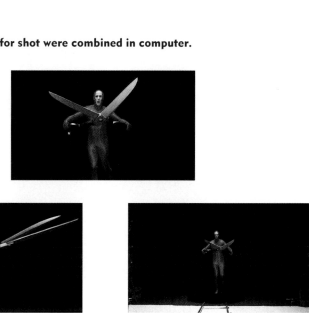

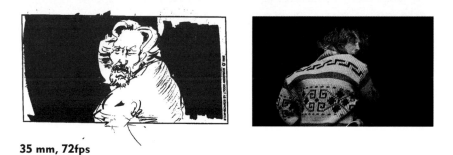

35 mm, 72fps

Following is a series of shots that were not storyboarded for various reasons.

- The 2-shot of the Dude and the Big Lebowski was a shot devised while blocking the scene on the location, suggested by Roger Deakins.

- The pulling shots of the Dude and Brandt were simply forgotten during the storyboarding sessions but were always intended, to complement the boarded POV of the Big Lebowski.

PULL Dude and Brandt into room
28mm

2-SHOT Dude and the Big Lebowski
28mm

PULL Dude and Brandt out of room
32mm

Many of the nonboarded shots in the Quintana sequence were suggested by wardrobe and props that Joel and Ethan had not seen at the time of storyboarding (e.g., insert of sock pull, insert of hands over hand dryer).

- The close-up of Quintana licking the bowling ball and the medium close-up of the hair net both came out of discussions with John Turturro.

- The 3-shot of Walter, Dude, and Donny came from blocking the scene: after watching the rehearsal, Joel and Ethan realized they wanted to bring the three characters into the montage sequence and create the feeling that the sequence was from their point of view.

- Panning Quintana back to the scoring table is the complement to the 3-shot.

INSERT – Quintana pulls up sock
35mm
48fps

INSERT – Quintana's hands over dryer
35mm
48fps

CLOSE-UP Quintana licking ball
50mm
96fps

MEDIUM CLOSE-UP Quintana's hair net
32mm
48fps

MEDIUM Quintana does victory jig
28mm
60 fps

Quintana's POV of O'Brian, PUSH IN
40mm
48fps

PAN Quintana to scoring table
135mm
48 fps

TRACK across Dude, Donny, and Walter
135mm
48fps

Suddenly, this otherwise murky tale of passion and murder flashes the cheerful, brightly lit image of Fred hurling a bowling ball down the hardwood with what can only be called balletic grace.

And, just as quickly, the moment is gone. Fred goes back to Babs for more of the old in-out-in-out, and gives her hubby the heave-ho, never to return to the comforts of kegling. The inexorable darkness closes in.

For that is the cruel law of bowling noir. Bowling is a bright beacon of chuckleheaded salvation burning in the dark existential American night, which noir characters can either follow to safety or spurn to wander forever lost. It is a symbol of goodness, wholesomeness, and tract housing—insipid, yes, even nightmarish in its own peculiar way, but rejected at one's own peril.

Put another way: bowl or die.

This is Fred MacMurray's lesson in *Double Indemnity*, and it is the lesson for Burt Lancaster in *Criss Cross* (1949), a bowling noir by virtue of the complete absence of bowling. Here, Burt is lured by

(continued)

alone end product with its own subjective content that is divorced from the process that made it.

"And so that's what we went for. Maude's splatter painting is an example. In keeping with Fluxus art technique, and evoking Maude's feminist views on sexuality, we went for depictions of body parts, either used as the brush or to move the paint around with. We also created splatter art in egg shapes as a portent of her plan to conceive with the Dude."

Armed with the Coens' mandate for indirectness, Rick soon found himself facing a challenge in the production design similar to the one Roger faced in the cinematography: finding a unifying visual theme in a panoply of willfully varying styles.

For Rick, the inspiration came from the film noir genre—though, of course, very indirectly.

Yvonne De Carlo into an ill-fated plot to hold up an armored car. Early in the doings, as the toothy, broad-shouldered one wavers between embracing the joys of family life and doing the same to Yvonne, Burt's father amiably suggests one night after dinner: "You wanna go bowling?"

Burt grins and shakes his head wryly. "I'm no bowler, Pop!" he says. With this, he has unwittingly pronounced his own death sentence. In a moral sense, the bowling noir universe is divided into those who "are bowlers" and those who "aren't bowlers."

A movie with a more redemptive spin on the theme, as well as being the most brazenly unabashed bowling noir of all time, is *Road House* (1948). In *Road House,* bowling is not just alluded to, it is the movie's very milieu: a flashy resort-town bowling center called Jefty's.

The story concerns a noirish love triangle between lonely soul-cum-bowling-center lounge singer Ida Lupino, lonely soul-cum-bowling-center manager Cornel Wilde, and perennial noir psychopath Richard Widmark.

Says Rick: "I'd done a lot of research on film noir and detective stuff in Hollywood and in L.A. for the *Fallen Angels* series. And I could see right from the beginning that *Lebowski* was a subversion of the genre. It was using aspects of noir, but populating it with Coen characters. These loser guys from the '60s applied to this very tried-and-true Holly-wood movie genre—the character of the Dude in all of these situations you've seen with Humphrey Bogart and Robert Mitchum.

"But, of course, the question then was, does that mean we try visually to evoke film noir imagery and somehow subvert it to present day and to these characters, or is it an oblique reference that they don't really want to make strongly? It's very important to Joe and Ethan that they not hit something right on the head. You don' go for the obvious. On the other hand, you don't want to be so obscure that the audience doesn't get it at all."

Says Ethan: "The noir element in the script didn't really seem t dictate anything stylistically in the movie. *The Big Lebowski* affects t

Here, bowling represents "the good life" and "settling down." As Cornel and Ida engage in the classic push-me-pull-you noir courtship, they shift between the seedy darkness and smoke of the bowling-center lounge to the clean, hopeful lights of the lanes as Cornel attempts to teach longtime single gal Ida "how to bowl." Structurally, the movie is all Ida's, as we follow her uplifting rehabilitation from independent, hard-as-nails hussy to what in the vernacular is known as an "avid bowler."

Bowling imagery abounds—from the saucy jazz montage of rumbling balls and two-tone shoes that opens the film, to the ubiquitous trophies and plaques that decorate the sets, to the nonstop clatter of off-screen tenpins that punctuates the drama like thunder in a horror flick.

Widmark goes psycho, of course, and some gunplay is involved, but in the end, bowling conquers all in *Road House.*

Here, a question arises—at some point, every student of the genre must ask it: if film noir's cinematic ancestry lies in the curious mar-

(continued)

be noir, but, in fact, it's a happy movie. It's a comedy. So, while noir seemed to be the flavor of the narrative, with all these characters trapped by their pasts, it was not the look of the movie. Certainly we didn't want it to look like a noir—for one thing, real noir is black-and-white. Consistent with the whole bowling thing, we wanted to keep the movie pretty bright and poppy."

And yet, noir did influence the look of the movie—in a very sneaky way.

"A lot of film noir have very simple sets," says Rick. "You can see really cheesy tapelines on walls and stuff like that. But the way they are shot and the way they are lit is very expressionistic. It is from that German expressionistic side that the composition and the way you light it express the emotion of the scene.

"So, with that in mind, what we concentrated on was giving Joel and Ethan and Roger interesting visual elements by which they could possibly create shadows, and by giving them foreground elements to shoot or not. The point was to keep everything appropri-

riage of German expressionist cinema and the American gangster movie, from which side comes the bowling?

Don't bother scanning *The Cabinet of Dr. Caligari* for scenes of a black-clad Conrad Veidt rolling cubes down a skewed lane. The answer lies in the early gangster classic *Scarface* (1932), specifically the scene in which Paul Muni, in his vicious crusade to wipe out his enemies, guns down Boris Karloff as he happily bowls at the local lanes. It is a shocking moment, illustrative of Muni's ruthless ambition and utter disregard for all that is sacred. Such blasphemy, of course, cannot go unpunished in bowling noir; by the final reel, Muni gets his, but good. Still, the ball had been set in motion in *Scarface*, and when the gangster flick mutated to create full-blown film noir, the bowling gene was there.

By the 1960s, bowling noir had all but played itself out, and there would be only one more entry of note. In *Cape Fear* (1962), Bob Mitchum as the malevolent and irrepressible ex-con Max Cady stalks Greg Peck and family. So malevolent and irrepressible is Bob he

ate and yet give them enough elements to play with on the set."

But something else emerged from Rick's thoughtful meditations on the expressionistic side of noir and its applications to *The Big Lebowski:* a recurring design motif, an image that would tie the various sets together, appearing either hopeful or malevolent, according to the scene's emotional subtext. It would appear most prominently in the bowling alley and then radiate outward, aesthetically speaking, onto other sets (or as many as the production's locations-heavy shoot would allow), even as the movie's plot itself radiated from this central location fixture in the life of the Dude.

The motif itself was a radiating icon.

And, for a story about L.A., an exquisitely apt one.

It was a star.

Says Ethan: "Since the bowling alley is sort of a linchpin, visuall' speaking, we discussed it with Rick more than any other set— although it was a practical location, not a set. The exterior of th

actually follows the family on an outing to the bowling center—a violation Greg later recounts with eyebrow-bobbing, tooth-whistling Peckian indignation to pal Martin Balsam: "You have to know him to feel the threat. He stopped me this afternoon after court, and he showed up again this evening at the *bowling* center!" Balsam is flabbergasted. Clearly, they are dealing with a madman.

By the time *Cape Fear* came along, however, the varnish on the old "bowling center as desecrated sanctuary" lane was well worn. The bowling noir genre had returned to its *Scarface* roots. The cycle was complete.

But now, with the arrival of *The Big Lebowski,* a new cycle begins.

Just as the arrival of the Coens' *Blood Simple* in 1984 marked the reemergence of film noir in the moviegoing vernacular and paved the way for an entire generation of independent filmmakers similarly inclined, *The Big Lebowski* promises to do the same for bowling noir.

Film noir; bowling noir. Even the coolest of genres may be burdened with an idiot son. ∎

place was just one big, solid, unbroken wall. So we talked about what to do with that. Rick came up with the idea of just laying free-form neon stars on top of it and doing a similar free-form star thing on the interior. It worked for a couple of reasons. One, it was cheaper than painting the whole exterior wall, but it also dovetailed nicely with the dream sequences"—both of which feature cosmic or astral backdrops combined with bowling imagery. "I don't know, it just started seeming right, his accents in the bowling alley."

Says Rick: "The interior of the bowling alley location was originally mauve and brown in a pattern of gradating bold stripes, which we painted over, more or less repeating the same kind of spectral pattern, but in orange and cream tones. I didn't want to go too nuts in there, painting-wise, since part of the whole budgetary thing was to please ourselves, but also please the owners so that we wouldn't have to spend the time and money restoring the place to its original mauve-and-brown state. But I also kept things very controlled on the walls, because I wanted to hang the blue free-form stars on top of that.

"Bowling alleys are all about radiating lines," says Rick. "There's something very optimistic about putting stars in that environment. The name of the bowling alley we used was even the Hollywood Star Lanes. It all just seemed so perfect. Also, stars are a very '50s thing, which worked well with that '50s-'60s Brunswick look the place had."

"People keep mentioning the 'Brunswick look,'" I say. "What is that look?"

"Brunswick is a bowling company," says Rick. "And in the '50s there was a certain color of orange and red that they used with a sort of beigey white that was fabulously reminiscent of the era that we were trying to evoke here. The ball returns and the overhead projection scoring tables all had a very space-agey, streamline look. A kind of Googie style."

Oh, Jesus.

"Googie?" I ask.

Rick pulls down a book from the shelf, and there it is, by Go right on the book's cover: Googie. Googie, I learn, is the initial derogatory but eventually affectionate nickname for a commerci style of architecture that appeared throughout the 1950s and ea 1960s, when new building technologies developed during WW were applied to peace (more or less) times. Thus, along the rapidly developing strip developments radiating (say . . .) out from the urban center toward the rapidly developing suburbs, small boxy commercial structures began to pop up, often made mostly of glass and pressed concrete made to resemble stone, and supporting angled roofs that jutted with rocket-aged, gravity-defying wonder high into the air.

"Great-looking, swooping architecture," says Rick. "When they realized because of new building techniques they could put a huge piece of concrete way up in the air, making it any shape they wanted to, everyone went crazy. It's the Jetsons look. The Flint-stones, too, actually, in a stone-agey kind of way. It was a look very common to coffee shop rest-aurants and bowling alleys back then—and it influenced the Brunswick look of that time, which is the era of the bowling alley we used."

I nod and clear my throat. "But getting back to the star motif—"

"Right—so the star motif is at its strongest and most optimistic in the bowling alley," says Rick, "but both dream sequences involve star patterns and are about lines radiating to a point, which is basically what a star is. In the first dream sequence the Dude gets knocked out and you see stars and they all coalesce into the overhead night-scape of L.A. The second dream sequence is an astral environment with a backdrop of stars and forced-perspective sets exaggeratedly diminishing into points.

"But we played with it in other ways, too," he continues. "For instance, in the Dude's bungalow, which was a constructed set, if you look at the ceiling, there's a similar pattern, created by the beams of the ceiling coming together, only it's moodier. I don't know that they actually shot up and saw it. I was hoping that when the Dude's listening to his headphones on the rug and he looks up and sees Maude and her assistant above him, that right before she knocks him out for the first dream sequence, you'd see a sort of luminous radiating pattern behind them. We also had a palm tree outside the window of the Malibu police chief's office, and palm fronds are a starlike pattern. But that's a very film noir, very expressionistic thing to do."

Rick concludes: "I mean, you really don't want to hit it too hard. You have to allow people to get it if they want and if not, that's okay, too. If you want, you can sort of after-the-fact rationalize it, come up with all kinds of analysis that makes it sound like a grand intellectual construction. But what it is, essentially, is just a motif. You conceive of or stumble onto motifs as you go, and you use those to link up the scenes. It's something to hang your hat on."

Though, in the case of *The Big Lebowski*, the mixture of bowling and noir is abstracted to the point of possibly being untraceable, the idea of commingling the bumptious, optimistic recreational activity of bowling with the brooding malevolence of film noir is not altogether unprecedented. Indeed, weird as it may seem, bowling as a quirky symbol of light and goodness contrastingly juxtaposed against the sinister goings-on of the dark, noir world is a lesser motif that runs throughout the genre's historic arc. It can be found in noir's gangster roots in *Scarface* (1932), in the genre's heyday in *Double Indemnity* (1944), *Road House* (1948), and, by way of dialogue, *Criss Cross* (1948), and, finally, in noir's declining years in *Cape Fear* (1962).

Bowling noir. I shit you negative. Go look them up. Fred MacMurray in bowling shoes, rolling a few, in between murder and sex with Barbara Stanwyck.

Still, as Rick says, such motifs are merely something to hang one's hat on.

Or are they?

But speaking of haberdashery . . .

Chapter 8

The Costume Design

Method Munsingwear

*C*ostume designing requires a unique blend of what ordinarily might be considered opposite character traits. On the one hand, it demands the "big picture" overview and grand-scale coordinating of a director. On the other hand, it requires an inward-looking, creative myopia that isn't too dissimilar from that of an actor who, while getting into his or her "method," obsessively contemplates the habits and lifestyle patterns of a character. The difference being, of course, that rather than gaining insight into the wear and tear on a character's psyche is the goal, for the costume designer, it is insight into the wear and tear on the character's pants.

At any rate, that was costume designer Mary Zophres's approach

Joel and Ethan with Mary Zophres.

to *The Big Lebowski*. Says Mary, perched among racks of clothes in the wardrobe trailer: "I wanted *The Big Lebowski* to look as naturalistic as possible, as opposed to having an overall 'designed look,' in which everybody has the same silhouette or the same color palate. For one thing, the dialogue was very real and the story was very character-driven. But I also didn't want the movie to feel 'designed,' because I think for smart-ass movies, which this definitely is, it's often a downfall if the smart-assness is too overbearing."

Mary Zophres grew up in Fort Lauderdale, Florida, and attended Vassar College, where she earned a B.A. in studio art and art history. While at Vassar, she took film classes, and by the time she graduated, Mary knew that she wanted to work in movies, but she wasn't certain exactly which department. Her first couple of film jobs were in art departments, but after working in the costume department on *Born on the Fourth of July*, she realized she'd found her niche.

Mary's first film with the Coen brothers was *Barton Fink*, thoug it was in the capacity of a production assistant and only for a month's tenure; in fact, it's difficult to say if she even laid eyes upon the Coens at all. After *Barton Fink*, however, Richard Hornung, the Coens' talented costume designer since *Raising Arizona*, whom Mary in fact had known pre-*Fink* in New York, hired Mary as his assistant. Together, they worked on such films as *This Boy's Life*, *Dave*, *Natural Born Killers*, and the Coens' *The Hudsucker Proxy*.

After seven years as an assistant, Mary herself ascended to the position of costume designer, working first on a low-budget comedy called *PCU*, then following it up, in a remarkable career leap, with the hit comedy *Dumb and Dumber*, in which she forever left her mark in the pantheon of comedic celluloid habilimentiers as the lively imagination behind Jim Carrey's and Jeff Daniels's gaudy tuxedos.

Before *Dumb and Dumber* hit the screens, however, the Coens were beginning pre-production on *Fargo*, and Richard Hornung, sick with AIDS, was forced to back out at the last minute. However, Richard recommended to Joel and Ethan a replacement: his one-time assistant Mary. To Mary, needless to say, it was a bittersweet turn. "I was thrilled to be asked to do it, but at the same time, the circumstances made it really sad and strange for me," she recalls.

Though Mary had worked on two previous Coen movies, her meeting with Joel and Ethan for *Fargo* was the longest conversation she'd had with them up until then. "When I sat down with them, they put me so at ease," she recalls. "I felt very comfortable with them. We talked about the script and, basically, found that we shared the same ideas. I thought I was just interviewing for the job; I went there with my portfolio, which they looked at. But it wasn't like I left the interview and they called later and said you have the job. While I was still there, they said, 'Well, we'd like you to do it.' And it was based on Richard's recommendation."

(You can spot Richard Hornung in *Miller's Crossing* as an extra, operating the flatbed machine gun outside the Sons of Erin, acting his heart out.)

———

As one might expect from the Coens' process, the costuming phase begins with a discussion.

Explains Joel: "With Mary, you discuss the characters. You go through the script character by character, discuss what you want each character to project, how you see each character, what you want them to look like. Sometimes you have very specific ideas about what you want them to wear and sometimes you have no idea. Mary then will work up sketches and ideas about what she wants, what she thinks the characters should wear based on what we've talked about. Then we sort of hash it out from there."

Says Mary: "I did maybe four sketches alone just of the Dude, indicating my ideas of different looks for him. 'This is the sort of shape I think he should wear,' and 'These are the kinds of clothes.' I don't sketch that well, but still, it's a definite springboard. It helps generate conversations. 'Yeah, this is right,' or 'No, this is way off.' Sometimes you're right on target and it's 'Yeah, that's great.'

"Then you get the cast. Then you start shopping or building the outfits. Then you get the actors in and start having fittings."

"How long does a fitting usually last?" I ask her.

"It depends. My first fitting with Jeff was two hours long. You usually don't want to go longer than that, because they can start to get faint and woozy. You bring in two racks of clothes, and at first you're just basically trying different things. It's just on-and-off and on-and-off, because you know pretty immediately whether something's going to work or not. Then you try putting things together. I always take 35mm pictures of my fittings to capture each thing that I think is worth showing to Joel and Ethan.

"With Jeff, we had several fittings with him, so we had lots of pictures. And rarely was there a specific ensemble from a fitting that ended up exactly like that on screen. It's like 'This could work here' and 'That could work there.'"

For some actors, says Mary, the wardrobe fitting can be a valued part of their preparation, as clothes choices are discussed at length in relation to the character. For others, a fitting is merely a fitting. The resulting on-screen performances, however, may be indistinguishable from one another. It's all a matter of an actor's approach to his or her craft.

"When an actor has a big part, I find a lot of times they like talking about it," says Mary. "John Goodman didn't want to talk about it at all. John felt he understood what the script was about, and if Joel and Ethan were happy with something and he felt good in it, then he was happy. Plus he told me he just doesn't like wardrobe fitting.

"But Jeff really enjoys the process of a fitting during the prep stage, seeing the different shapes on himself. Often he would bring into fittings suggested garments of his own. I think it helped him with the character."

In all, Mary had four or five fittings with Jeff Bridges before she began to narrow things down for the Dude's "style." "There's a quality of looseness, a quality of worn-in softness to the fabric and color choices," she says by way of description. "A washed-out quality. The Dude is somebody who may own a piece of clothing for ten years. And he doesn't separate his darks from his lights.

"I found that Jeff looked better in a baggier trouser than in a more tight-fitting trouser. It was just more the Dude. It was sloppier. And we found that it was good when things ran below his belly, because it emphasized that he was lazy and had a bit of a gut. I also found that Jeff is a broad-shouldered guy, so it worked better when his T-shirt skimmed his body, because you saw the outline of his stomach. But if you went too oversized with his top half, then it started to look trendy and a little too good. So with his T-shirts, we stuck with a closer-fitting one—not tight, but closer-fitting. Then whatever goes over that can be loose again.

"I've used a lot of drop shoulders on him because when somebody has higher seams, it somehow improves the posture and makes their look seem more put-together and tidy, which of course we didn't want."

Here, Mary pauses. "I know this all seems like a very subtle thing, but from a costume designer's point of view, it does make a difference. And if you make sure that you're doing it the right way down to the basics, then you're assured of getting the overall effect you want."

So. How basic does it get?

Can you say "Munsingwear"?

"The Dude wears Munsingwear underwear in the movie," says Mary, "which is a brand of tightie-whities that has been around for years. And it says its name on the band: 'Munsingwear.' It was a brand that Joel and Ethan thought was pretty humorous. You know, just the name: 'Munsingwear.' They liked that. It was definitely a starting point for the character."

"The underwear was?" I ask.

"Yeah," Mary says. "There was something very Dudesque about his wearing Munsingwear and letting the Munsingwear band stick up above his pants. Something very sloppy about it. And after our first fitting, when Jeff knew that Joel and Ethan liked the Munsingwear, he took a pair of Munsingwear home and started wearing his Munsingwear so he could get into character."

"Just the one pair?" I say.

Mary ignores me. "Actually, I love working with actors like Jeff, because they get so into the costuming. The fittings really help them get into character."

She goes on: "Now the fact that the Dude lives in Venice definitely influenced our approach to him. I wanted him to have a feeling of beachiness about him. I tried to shop for him, but we ended up building a lot of his stuff, because we needed multiples"—stunt double garments, in which the stunts entail coffee spills or bloodstains. "But the inspiration for all his stuff came from things that we shopped for in the beach area."

Here, Mary relays the story of the flip-flops and the jellies: "I originally wanted the Dude to wear flip-flops, because I thought it would be a really cool thing to have a 'keelunk-keelunk' sound every time he came into a room. And I was obsessed with flip-flops for the first week. But when I met with Jeff, it turned out he had a bad back and couldn't do the whole movie in flip-flops.

"Then one day Jeff wore jellies [translucent plastic sandals] into a fitting. He had worn them on, I guess, *White Squall,* or maybe they were his off-camera shoes—they were basically ship shoes. But they were very beachy and really perfect. Jellies were actually very popular in the early '90s and now are impossible to find. We had to go to Trinidad for those stupid jellies. You'd think it'd just be 'O yeah, somebody go to K Mart and buy the jellies,' but they are nowhere to be found. Except for ones with heels, for women.

"The jellies were Jeff's idea, and it was a really good solution. I felt the Dude's clothes should be a little off-kilter, a bit odd—and that's what the jellies were, even more so than the flip-flops. And so I let go of the flip-flops and became obsessed with the jellies. Jeff was always asking if he could wear other shoes, and I was always, like, 'Please wear your jellies.' I loved the jellies."

"In the movie," Mary says, "there are two long changes—days that take up like twenty scenes or something. When I say 'change,' I mean literally every time he changes his clothes. His change one, his change two, his change three. These changes take place according to when the sun is coming up and going down in the context of the movie. When the sun goes up or down, of course, is something determined by Joel and Ethan and the script supervisor. And when one of those days lasts through a whole bunch of scenes, and he's going to be wearing the same outfit for a long time on-screen, I call them long changes, though I don't know if that's the proper terminology."

The Dude has two long changes during *The Big Lebowski*, and consideration of those two long "days" was a big part of putting together the character's overall wardrobe, says Mary. "When I looked at the script days and broke down the Dude's changes," she says, "I went to Joel and Ethan and asked, 'Is this how we want to do the Dude? Or do we want to have him change his clothes somewhere along the way so we don't have to see him in the same clothes for all this time?' And they said, 'No, he should be in the same clothes.'"

In determining the ensemble for a long change, other people must be brought into the decision, says Mary. "Jeff has to wear it a long time. Joel and Ethan have to stare at it a long time. And if there are special considerations as far as cinematography goes, Roger has to be consulted. During the first long change, for example, there was a lot of night shooting and Roger said he'd rather not have the Dude in one of his white T-shirts because of how that would affect the lighting."

Also, the Dude repeats a few articles of clothing during the course of the story the way people in real life do, and that factors into the long change as well. And not only do you have to decide what the Dude will wear for the twenty-scene day, but the wardrobe of the other actors then must be selected in such a way that they do not unintentionally clash or jibe with the Dude's duds. In this last concern, Joel and Ethan's comprehensive approach to storyboarding comes into play.

Says Mary: "What the Dude is wearing in a scene does play a role in determining what the other characters wear. With Joel and Ethan, however, that job is easier because you just look at the storyboard and you know exactly how the characters are going to be positioned in the frame and you can say, 'Okay, I'm going to put him in this color because he's going to be right next to the Dude and he can't wear this other shirt, because the Dude is in this shirt.'"

The Dude, being the hero, of course, is the most critical individual character in *The Big Lebowski* for whom Mary and her crew must build a wardrobe; certainly he is the most intensive and involving. But it's important, if not astonishing, to realize that essentially the same process is used in clothing every other character in the movie, no matter how small the role.

"With Walter," says Mary, "we just went with the idea of him as presented in the script, which is that he talks about Vietnam all the time. But I didn't want to put him in fatigues all the time, because that would have been a bit overboard and too obvious. In the script, it says that he wears a shirt with cutoff sleeves, but in my first meeting with Joel and Ethan, we came up with the idea of a pocketed fisherman's vest."

"What made you decide to change it?" I ask.

"I wanted to suburbanize Walter a bit," Mary says. "He's a big, rough guy, but at the same time, John Goodman has such a sweet face. A lot of it had to do with John being the actor cast in the role

When we first started pulling stuff for him, it was much more mili-tary-inspired, like T-shirts and some thermals, but in army colors. Then as we had our first fitting with John, I realized that there was something I liked about mixing it up a little bit, and suburbanizing the military element. And I think it works.

"Walter's glasses are very key, I think, and that I found through research," she continues. "I was doing research on Vietnam veter-ans and there was this guy, I swear to God, he had a brush haircut almost exactly like the one John wears as Walter—though his went a little forward and John's goes up. But he had on these glasses. They're antiglare glasses like pilots wear, with that teardrop shape. There is something really awful about them, something very intense. Whenever you see Walter wearing them, you're reminded of that intensity. And it was something Joel and Ethan really liked."

She goes on: "Aside from that, there are just a few times when the Dude and Walter go out on 'missions', and for those we had Walter get geared up in something special. When they go to Arthur Digby Sellers's house with the homework in a baggie, Walter wears suit to go conduct the investigation, because he feels his shorts are so informal for something like that. And when they go to drop off the ransom money, we had him get suited up in his old army jacket and army pants, with a bandanna around his head."

And what of the fair Maude Lebowski, the Dude's *objet d'amour?*

"When I first read the script, I wanted an eccentric look for Maude," Mary says. "My first thought was to dress her like the Lava Lady, who is this crazy woman who walks the streets around La Brea and Melrose. She wears her hair tied up in a bun and pointed in the shape of a unicorn and she wears velvet all in one color. There is a rumor that she is an artist and she lives in a black house and that's why they call her the Lava Lady."

"Huh," I nod.

"And I remember Joel and Ethan's vision of Maude was that she should be in high collars and long lengths and have something regal about her," she says. "But there were other things that figured in as well. When the Dude goes to visit her in her loft, she's doing her Fluxus painting thing flying back and forth in a harness, and when she gets down you need to have something she can just slip right on. In the script, it's a robe. Well, we only see her a few times, and you want to keep her silhouette, her overall look, sort of the same and not change it too much. That's what led us to scrap any idea of real clothes for her. We ended up saying, okay, if we have her in a robe shape for after she paints, then let's have another kind of robe shape when she knocks the Dude out, and that ended up being a cape. She wears nothing underneath it except for a pair of knee-high boots.

"But as far as the high collar went, we sort of split the difference. This is where you take the ideas of the director, the ideas of the costume designer, and the physical realities of the actor. Julianne was really interested in having the character be eccentric, but she had a problem with the high collars next to her neck, so we lowered it to the point that she was comfortable, but then angled it so as to capture the illusion of a high collar. In fact, in the end, when she gets down from the harness, we ended up not having the robe at all and she just puts on the cape. The cape is really great, actually—I love it. It's one of my favorite costumes in the movie."

And then, as they say, there are the nihilists. But not just nihilists: nihilists of radically varying heights.

Says Mary: "In the script it says that the nihilists are in head-to-toe black leather, and I thought, okay, I'll just dress them in head-to-toe black leather. But Joel and Ethan were very specific in saying, 'You know, we don't want them to be in leather all the time. Black is fine, but the only time we want them in leather jackets and leather pants is when they're with their bikes or at the end, burning the Dude's car.' Joel and Ethan wanted them in leather only in association with the bikes. If we didn't see the bikes, we weren't going to put them in leather."

"Why was that such a concern?" I ask.

"They didn't want it to look West Hollywood leather bar–ish," says Mary. "The look of the nihilists is meant to be more of a punk influence than leather, like they're caught in a time warp from the '80s. To drive that home, most of the time the nihilists are wearing black. I didn't dress anybody else in the movie in black except for the nihilists. Their accent color is red. If they had any color in their wardrobe at all, it usually was a red accent."

Mary continues: "With regard to their silhouettes, I was very specific with what I wanted. I wanted really spiked legs. I wanted all their pants to be really slim-fitting all the way down to big boots to create this threatening, Frankenstein-type silhouette. I loved the scale of the three of them, so I tried to play with that a lot, because I knew, with the exception of Uli, they'd always be in the same frame together, creating a 'little bear, middle bear, and big bear' effect, because their heights are so different.

"Also, Joel told me that the idea behind the nihilists was that they were probably wealthy about ten years before, when they had their German techno-pop group, Autobahn, which for the script would've been in the early '80s," says Mary, "and that's when they bought a lot of their clothes. But now, in the presentday of the movie, those clothes are practically threadbare. So we really aged the clothing amazingly. Not homeless-type aging, but really thread-bare."

Here, Mary provides an entertaining clothing-related nihilist anecdote. "I gave one of the nihilists, Flea, hip huggers," Mary recalls. "They were actually original '70s pants. I didn't want them to look '70s, but I loved the hip length, so I made them pegged, tapering them at the calf, so he could wear them in his boots.

"Well, in the big fight scene at the end in the bowling alley parking lot, the scene calls for him to crawl across the pavement. Cookie Lopez, one of my set costumers, was covering him on set for that scene, and she noticed that his pants were lowering as he crawled and you could see his butt crack. So she's over there, trying to lift his pants up and make it so his butt's covered, and Joel and Ethan saw it and they got excited. They told Cookie to stop and told Flea to arch his back more and stick his butt higher in the air as he crawled to emphasize it. So in the scene, hopefully, as he crawls, you'll see his little butt crack hovering above his head.

"It was one of those magical things that just happens," she says, "but it was hilarious."

Here my chat with Mary about the nihilists raises a larger issue.

No, not the meaning of life.

Rather, the aging of clothes through artificial means. With so many characters trapped in so many different clothing-represente pasts, *The Big Lebowski* involved quite a bit of clothes-aging.

"What do you do to clothes to age them?" I ask.

"It depends on what it is," says Mary. "Anything from heavy-duty sanding to using cheese graters and dirt, washing tons of times. The dirt is actually theater dirt, a clean dirt that comes in different colors and you mix it with some oils and you can create a nice dinge. We also found wall washer works really well to break clothes down. It's called TSP—I use that all the time. We were constantly using sanders on clothes. You just speed up the process of what normally happens in a ten-year span of time. Breaking it down, then sanding, then washing, then sanding, then washing. But it is time-consuming to do it properly."

She continues: "One of the keys to the Dude's clothes was that they could not look brand-new. So everything he has we sanded from the inside, because that helps make everything droop and sag. Let's say he wears this sweatshirt. When I got this thing, it was brand-new because I needed multiples of it, so it was thick and stiff like any new sweatshirt, so we sanded it on the inside and washed and sanded and pretty soon, all the fuzz was off and we destroyed the entire inner layer. And it went from being this stiff new sweatshirt to this saggy, droopy old thing. You can't buy multiples like that from a thrift store. You have to buy them new and age them."

"How long did that take?" I ask.

"The sweatshirt took a week to age," she says. "But there were six of them. So we aged six sweatshirts over the course of a week. While we were in prep we had two people doing nothing but aging, because so many of the characters' clothing in the movie had to be aged.

"And they often needed multiples, or their measurements made it impossible to find anything in a thrift store. Like Torsten, who plays one of the nihilists, is six feet nine and I couldn't find anything in a thrift store, so all his clothes had to be bought brand-new and aged. The same thing with Walter. John's vest was something we had to build, because in reality, it didn't exist in his size. So we made six of them, then we started breaking them all down.

"I don't know that other designers age clothes as much as I do. But I find it to be a very important step before sending something to the camera. Because it really helps to make clothes look realistic. To send something before the cameras that is not aged just makes it stand out."

Getting back to the characters, thus far, we have dealt primarily with costume design as it pertains to characters who . . . well, have character. But what of those about whom the script offers virtually nothing in the way of character direction? Yeah, yeah, sure—it's hard for the actor and all. But Jesus—how do you *dress* 'em?

Such was the predicament with a character who, for exactly this reason, we have not discussed much in this book: the Dude's and Walter's ever-present but always ignored teammate, Donnie (Steve Buscemi), at whom Walter is forever hurling belittlements and instructions to "shut the fuck up."

With Donnie, Mary was left to invent all on her own.

Says Mary: "Donnie was a tough one, because he doesn't say much. So I spent a lot of time trying to get a handle on him. He seems to always be looking for someone else's opinion and someone else's approval, or he's literally just asking what someone else has said.

"So I thought, okay, this is just somebody who loves to bowl. He's been following the careers of bowlers and reading up and researching bowlers for as long as he's been bowling, and this is how he has chosen to spend his time—to dress like original bowlers in old-fashioned bowling shirts."

Mary goes on: "So in my mind, he had collected vintage bowling shirts through the years. He selects them very carefully and covers them in plastic and takes pretty good care of them. But at the same time I wanted him to sort of look like a sad sack, so we made it so that everything we got for Donnie was a couple of sizes too large—pants, shirts. Steve Buscemi is small and I've worked with him before on *Fargo*, so I knew his body shape and I knew what happened when he put clothes on that were too big or too small."

Which is all well and good—but what of crowd scenes, composed of completely anonymous people who are not even specifically mentioned in the script? What about, say, the background actor portraying the other bowlers in the bowling alley? In such an instance, Mary must think about the style and clothing motivations of not just a handful of fictional characters, but of the entire indoor recreational community of the geographic area where that handful of fictional characters hypothetically thrive. When you're talking those kinds of numbers, suddenly the costume designer's job description, more than anything, resembles that of an anthropologist.

"I went to a couple of bowling alleys and just watched how people dressed," explains Mary. "At first I assumed that this bowling alley was supposed to be the closest one to the Dude's house, which is in Venice, which would have made it the Mar Vista Bowl. But as a rule, you don't want to have your extras dressing like your principles, so I decided not to put it in Venice, because there'd be a bunch of Dude types walking around.

"Then I started thinking," she continues. "Maybe they do some traveling to get there, maybe it's more nondescript. Maybe they bowl in the Valley, some place that the Dude could get to quickly on the 405, because Walter, I imagine, probably lives in the Valley. So then I thought, this one, in reality, is a much more ethnic clientele than the Mar Vista. It's a bit of a middle-American kind of place. I wanted there to be a cross section of life in the bowling alley."

Now.

With the hope of better illustrating just how the Coen Process works in practice, each of the next four chapters will examine a scene from *The Big Lebowski*. Following the script pages and a narrative explanation of the scene that sets it in its proper Lebowskian context, there will be comments about the scene from Joel and Ethan, Roger, Rick, and Mary.

At the back of the book, one will find corresponding color plates to each scene that document quite nicely each scene's evolution from storyboard, to costume sketches, to framed celluloid image.

So . . . maybe the next section will help you to understand.

God knows we've tried everything else.

Chapter 9

The Great-Room Scene

The Detritus of a Rich Man
Or
Babe Ruth, the Sadaharu Oh of American
Baseball

Scene 16

INT. LEBOWSKI MANSION—GREAT ROOM—NIGHT

Brandt throws open a pair of heavy double doors. The music washes over us as we enter a great study where Jeffrey Lebowski, a blanket thrown over his knees, stares hauntedly into a fire, listening to "LOHENGRIN."

Brandt announces, ambiguously:

BRANDT

Mr. Lebowski.

Jeffrey Lebowski waves the Dude in without looking around.

                    LEBOWSKI
. . . It's funny. I can look back on a life of
achievement, on challenges met, competitors best-
ed, obstacles overcome . . . I've accomplished
more than most men, and without the use of my
legs. What . . . What makes a man, Mr. Lebowski?

                    DUDE
Dude.

                    LEBOWSKI
. . . Huh?

                    DUDE
I don't know, sir.

                    LEBOWSKI
Is it . . . is it, being prepared to do the right
thing? Whatever the price? Isn't that what makes a
man?

                    DUDE
Sure. That and a pair of testicles.

Lebowski turns away from the Dude with a haunted stare,
lost in thought.

                    LEBOWSKI
. . . You're joking, but perhaps you're right . . .

                    DUDE
Mind if I smoke a jay?

                    LEBOWSKI
. . . Bunny . . .

122

He turns back around and the firelight shows teartracks on his cheeks.

                    DUDE
     'Scuse me?

                    LEBOWSKI
     . . . Bunny Lebowski . . . She is the light of my
     life. Are you surprised at my tears, sir?

                    DUDE
     Fuckin' A.

                    LEBOWSKI
     Strong men also cry . . . Strong men also cry . . .

He clears his throat.

                    LEBOWSKI (CONTINUING)
     . . . I received this fax this morning.

Brandt hastily pulls a flimsy sheet from his clipboard and hands it to the Dude.

                    LEBOWSKI (CONTINUING)
     . . . As you can see, it is a ransom note. Sent by
     cowards. Men who are unable to achieve on a level
     field of play. Men who will not sign their names.
     Weaklings. Bums.

The Dude examines the fax:

     WE HAVE BUNNY. GATHER ONE MILLION DOLLARS IN
     UNMARKED, NONCONSECUTIVE TWENTIES. AWAIT INSTRUC-
     TIONS. NO FUNNY STUFF.

                    DUDE
     Bummer.

Lebowski looks soulfully at the Dude.

                    LEBOWSKI
    . . . Brandt will fill you in on the details.

He wheels his chair around once again to gaze into the fire.
Brandt tugs at the Dude's shirt and points him back to the
hall.

*T*he great-room scene marks the Dude's second visit to the Lebowski mansion. It is quite different in tone from the first visit, in which the Dude makes a pilgrimage to seek recompense for his wrongly peed upon rug. In this initial daytime meeting with the rotund, three-piece-suited, wheelchair-implanted Big Lebowski, the Dude finds both his petition and himself greeted with hostility, and Lebowski chases him out, berating the stunned Duderino for so unexaminedly treading the freeloader's lifestyle path.

Departing, the Dude informs the Big Lebowski's assistant, Brandt, that the tycoon has told him to take any rug in the house. As Brandt, the Dude, and the houseman lug the Dude's new, expensive, but more importantly urine-free rug past the swimming pool, the Dude encounters the Big Lebowski's sexually non-exclusive wife, Bunny, and her nihilist pal, Uli, who bobs stuporously alongside an empty whiskey bottle, in an inflatable pool chair.

Thus endeth the Dude's first visit to the Lebowski mansion.

However, here, in the Dude's second visit, dubbed the great-room scene, the tone is more somber—bathetically so, really, as the Dude, with assurances from Brandt that the boosted rug is not an issue, is summoned back to the Lebowski mansion at night and ushered into the great room. There the Dude finds the Big Lebowski sitting in darkness, gazing into a fire, listening to Wagner's *Lohengrin,* and weeping unabashed tears. After waxing philosophic about the nature of manhood, the bereft millionaire reveals that clutched in his hand is a faxed ransom note informing

the faxee, him, that his beloved wife, Bunny, has been kidnapped.
Then he dismisses the Dude.

Out in the hallway, the Dude is enlisted by Brandt to act as bagman in the $1 million ransom transaction. Since, the Dude is told,
the Big Lebowski's operating assumption is that the kidnappers and
the Dude's rug befoulers are one and the same, as part of the Dude's
bagman responsibilities, he must confirm the kidnappers' identity.

For his trouble, Brandt offers the Dude a generous fee. Presum-
ably, it is the Dude's first paying job in years.

ETHAN   "It's a great-room scene. In a great room, you traditional-
ly have stuffed animal heads and, you know, a fire. This is a
tycoon. He's in retreat. So, you know, he's going to have a comforter over his legs and he has to be staring into the fire. A great
affliction is being visited upon him in the kidnapping of his wife.
Everything follows from that. A great man, meditating, staring
hauntedly into the fire.

"This is cinematic child's play. I mean, give it to any hack TV
director and they'll say, 'Oh, sure, great room. Well, we'll need a
comforter for his knees and he'll need to be staring into the fire.'

"A great-room scene. We've done them before. We'll do them again.

JOEL   "We like great-room scenes for some reason: guys sitting in front of fires with blankets over their knees.

"I remember when we were shooting it, Jeff being very interested in the ceiling—you know, checking out the ceiling—and that became kind of a thing that the Dude did in a lot of different locations: whenever he came into a new space, he would check the ceilings out. Whether or not it's actually going to come through in the movie or if we use those takes, I don't know yet. I hope it does.

"Also there was a brief blocking discussion about how the Dude tends to go into spaces and he gets pretty comfortable pretty fast and how exactly he might get comfortable in that space. Originally, we sort of imagined him standing there, but with the first blocking rehearsal, Jeff wanted to perch or kind of lean on the edge of the couch."

ROGER   "The source of light in the room was to be the fire and the firelight. But the firelight itself was nowhere near enough to illuminate the room—you had to put some sort of lighting effect in there to simulate the fire.

"The way it was storyboarded, from the Dude's point of view, you come into the room and you track completely around the Big Lebowski as he stares into the fire, which sort of negated being able to source him from there, because you wouldn't be able to get anything in the hearth to boost the firelight and not have it be seen.

"The fireplace in this location wasn't a big one to begin with. It was tiny. That's why I say the location dictates what you can do. If it had been bigger, I could have probably done a gag that you could have tracked right across anyway, but that was the restriction of the location. We could've maybe found another location that was slightly better suited, but then that would have cost money. We didn't have that prep time. With a location, it's always a compromise.

"So, although it was storyboarded as one shot, we did this in two pieces. We never actually shot square on towards the fireplace, and that way I could hide something in the hearth. I made up a special unit to fit in there—a reflective sheet of aluminum with one-and-a-half-kilowatt bulbs on there, dimming, pulsing, wavering to give a slightly firelight effect.

"Then we just got a shot of Jeff walking into the room as the cut between the two pieces, so you think it's one move. And obviously, once the camera's shooting away from the fire, you've got the space to bring in light and dummy the effect the way you want.

"There's one little insert there—where Jeff's looking at the ransom note. We made it look as though Jeff was reading the ransom note backlit by the fire rather than by shedding a light source on it. On the shot towards Jeff, he holds the ransom note up and his face goes into shadow. Then you cut around and you see that the thing's backlit and illuminated by the fire. A little thing that I thought was rather nice."

RICK   "It was hard finding the right place. Joel and Ethan wanted to shoot the interior Lebowski mansion scenes—the hallway, the study, and the great room—in one location, more or less at one time. It's always good if you can keep sequences together and in order, rather than jumping around to different locations, because you've got better control that way, and it allows the actor to develop the scene better.

"But we needed it to have that grand feeling you get when you're looking at, for example, General Sternwood's place in *The Big Sleep*. You needed to feel that the walls just go up and up; everything you're looking at—the pictures on the wall, the people—should feel small in comparison. You want a bit of a *Citizen Kane* feeling, to make a strong statement about this pitiful guy in a wheelchair with all this magnificent artwork staring down at him. As filmmakers, Joel and Ethan are very attuned to contrasts, and if you had the pathetic character of the Big Lebowski in his wheelchair but the room wasn't contrasting him proportionally, the scene would be a lot less strong.

"We weren't liking the mansion pictures we were seeing because there was no scale to them. I didn't feel confident that we would ever be able to find something that satisfied our needs. I was pretty confident we'd find a study, but I wasn't confident we'd find a great room, and I was beginning to think we should build the great room on a stage.

"The decision whether to build a set or shoot on location is a budgetary one that depends on a variety of factors, such as how long a shoot you're planning for the given set and what kind of deal exists for the stage on which it's built. Basically, it's easier to build a set, so a lot of film companies just do that automatically. The advantage is that you can build it exactly the way you want it to look, and you don't have to worry about weather or day/night concerns. Of course, it's also more money.

"In this case, we determined it was cheaper to shoot on location. And what's good about shooting on location is that a lot of the stuff you need is already there, so you save money. But there are some restrictions to doing it that way—physical restrictions. Which is why I say that a lot of design is about embracing reality.

"Although the mansion we ended up using satisfied our needs, one thing that was wrong with the place was the hallway floor. It had this black-and-white-checkered marble tile floor. Joel hated the look. He said it looked like a men's room and they should line up urinals along the wall. From the beginning we were trying to figure out how to cover up the floor, which is a pretty big task. One thought was to do a scenic tile job—actually painting our own tile—and completely tiling over the place. But we couldn't be confident, for those long shots looking down the hallway, that you wouldn't see something popping up somewhere. After a certain point, we decided that our options were either too expensive or too uncertain, so we should just shoot the way it was.

"I was also disappointed by the fireplace. It was very small. But it was already there and we were told we couldn't do anything with it.

"Overall, I liked the great room. It's the sort of place where you have your midnight of the soul. In the firelight you catch glimpses of tapestry and sculpture and there is a lot of nubile nymph sculpture in there to remind you of your trophy wife.

"Since the mansion was empty and is just used for movies, we completely set-dressed the great room. We brought in all of the drapery, all of the tapestry, all of the paintings, all of the furniture, all of the rugs, everything except what you can't walk away with. It looks like it was built by someone who just wanted it to look grand, a rich person without too much taste. Lots of cheesy French paintings. The detritus of a rich man—we wanted that kind of feeling."

MARY "This is the scene in which the Big Lebowski is in his black smoking jacket. We chose that because he was crying and sort of pathetic and yet was wearing clothing meant to make him look debonair. The contrast between his being in this puffed-up outfit, trying to appear sort of grand, while he's sobbing—there's just something sort of hilarious about that.

"Whenever the Big Lebowski is not wearing his three-piece suit, as is the case here, we put him in ascots. There is a peacock quality about him. He is affected and he believes his lie himself. He dresses the part that he professes to be, but really isn't.

"Brandt—poor Brandt—is always in a suit, and that's just the way he is, because we only see him at work and he doesn't go to work relaxed. We kept him very American, meaning his suit shoulders weren't too big, and he cut a very conservative silhouette—very preppie. I dressed him like Ralph Reed, the former head of the Christian Coalition: gray suits, Brooks Brothers white button-down-collar shirts, and preppie repetitive-motif ties.

"Now, the silly shirt that the Dude is wearing is actually copied from a shirt Jeff showed us. In our first meeting with Jeff, he brought it in his trunk. It's an undersleeve shirt—a baseball shirt that they wear under their uniform—with contrasting sleeves. It had a Japanese baseball player on the front of it and his name in Japanese above him." (In fact, it was Sadaharu Oh, considered the Babe Ruth of Japanese baseball, and, one would presume for the Japanese, vice versa.) "I thought it was hilarious. So, we copied it.

"As we were figuring out the Dude's look, we were trying to figure out where to place that shirt. To me, Jeff looked really stupid in the shirt—he looked, like, "AHHH-DUHHH!" in it. So to me, the great-room scene was the most appropriate place, because the Dude so doesn't know what's going on. They're pulling the wool over his eyes.

"The reason he's wearing those particular pants is because I wanted to repeat clothes on the Dude. Meaning, he doesn't have that many clothes, and he tends to pick them up off the floor, smell them, and if they don't reek, put them on again. There are other scenes where he repeats clothes quite a bit."

The Coen brothers have an earlier great-room scene in *Miller's Crossing*. The tycoon-cum-homebody in that flick is gangster psychopath Johnny Caspar. And while the great-room scene in *Miller's Crossing* is a bit different tonally from the *Lebowski* great-room scene—there's a little more bellowing, a touch of attempted strangulation, some face-whacking with a shovel, and some brains being blown out—both great-room scenes are imbued with the unmistakable Coenesque great-room touch of a warm, cozy fire and a smoking jacket.

For storyboard trivia enthusiasts (of whom there may be a larger number than we as an advanced society would like to admit), there are a number of points of interest in this scene. In the medium close-up of the Dude, hanging on the wall behind him is a late eighteenth-century military self-portrait by storyboard artist J. Todd Anderson. Also, in the close-up insert of the ransom fax, J. Todd portrays the fax as having been issued from the "Hotel Earl," which after the relatively minor punctilious adjustment of adding an "e" to the end, is the name of the Deco-Gothic hotel at which Barton stays in *Barton Fink*.

The medium shot of Brandt in the storyboard shows him turned away, admiring the great room's statuary with his hands clasped behind his back, a depiction 180 degrees different from the way the set-up was actually shot. This, explains Ethan, is more than likely because in the throes of their storyboarding frenzy with J. Todd (and feeling perhaps that this shot was a good example of one of the "banal" bits of camera coverage about which Ethan spoke in an earlier chapter), the Coens told J. Todd little more than "medium shot on Brandt" before that lightning sketch was rendered and slapped onto the pile. A similar dynamic is no doubt behind the fact that set-up 6, 7 and 8 are sequentially transposed. These sorts of discrepancies occur in the process from time to time, and are hardly worth mentioning. So I won't again.

Of the fact that the storyboarded pull-back shot on the Big Lebowski is in reality nothing more than a duplication of the storyboarded tracking-in shot on him, with crudely scrawled arrows and circled letters attempting to fill in for good, hard, decent work, I have nothing to say.

Chapter 10

The Quintana Scene

Another Use for Birdseed

Scene 18

INT. BOWLING ALLEY—NIGHT
BOWLING PINS

CRASH—scattered by a strike, in slow motion.

WIDER

Still in slow motion. We are looking across the length of

133

the bowling alley at a tall, thin, Hispanic bowler (QUIN-
TANA) displaying perfect form. He wears an all-in-one
Dacron-polyester stretch bowling outfit with a racing stripe
down each side.

FAST TRACK IN

On the Dude, sitting next to Walter in the molded plastic
chairs. The Dude is staring off towards the bowler.

                         DUDE
    Fucking Quintana—that creep can roll, man—

BACK TO QUINTANA

Displaying great slow-motion form as the Dude and Walter's
conversation continues over.

                        WALTER
    Yeah, but he's a fucking pervert, Dude.

                         DUDE
    Huh?

                        WALTER
    The man is a sex offender. With a record. Spent
    six months in Chino for exposing himself to an
    eight-year-old.

Scene 19

EXT. VENICE NEIGHTBORHOOD—DAY—(FLASHBACK)

We see Quintana, in pressed jeans and a stretchy sweater,
walking up a stoop in a residential neighborhood and ring-

ing the bell. The voice over conversation continues.

                    DUDE (V.O.)

Huh.

                    WALTER (V.O.)
When he moved down to Venice he had to go door-to-
door to tell everyone he's a pedarast.

The door swings open and a beer-swilling middle-aged man
looks dully out at Quintana, who looks hesitantly up.

                    DONNY (V.O.)
What's a pedarast, Walter?

                    WALTER (V.O.)
Shut the fuck up, Donny.

Scene 20

INT. BOWLING ALLEY—NIGHT

PINS

scattered by strike.

QUINTANA

wheeling and thrusting a black gloved fist into the air.
stitched above the breast pocket of his all-in-one is his
first name, "Jesus."

BACK TO WALTER AND THE DUDE

They have been joined by Donny.

                         WALTER
          Anyway. How much they offer you?

                         DUDE
          Twenty grand. And of course I still keep the rug.

                         WALTER
          Just for making the hand-off?

                         DUDE
          Yeah . . .

He slips a little black box out of his shirt pocket.

                         DUDE (CONTINUING)
          . . . They gave Dude a beeper, so whenever these
          guys call—

                         WALTER
          What if it's during a game?

                         DUDE
          I told him if it was during league play—

Donny has been watching Quintana.

                         DONNY
          If what's during league play?

                         WALTER
          Life does not stop and start at your convenience,
          you miserable piece of shit.

                         DONNY
          What's wrong with Walter, Dude?

                         DUDE
          I figure it's easy money, it's all pretty harmless.

I mean she probably kidnapped herself.

                    WALTER
Huh?

                    DONNY
What do you mean, Dude?

                    DUDE
Rug-peers did not do this. I mean look at it.
Young trophy wife. Marries a guy for money but fig-
ures he isn't giving her enough. She owes money
all over town—

                    WALTER
That . . . fucking . . . bitch!

                    DUDE
It's all a goddam fake. Like Lenin said, look for
the person who will benefit. And you will, uh, you
know, you'll, uh, you know what I'm trying to say—

                    DONNY
I am the Walrus.

                    WALTER
That fucking bitch!

                    DUDE
Yeah.

                    DONNY
I am the Walrus.

                    WALTER
Shut the fuck up, Donny! *V.I.* Lenin! Vladimir
Ilyich *Ul*yanov!

                    DONNY
What the fuck is he talking about?

                         WALTER

That's fucking exactly what happened, Dude! That
makes me fucking SICK!

                          DUDE

Yeah, well, what do you care, Walter?

                         DONNY

Yeah, Dude, why is Walter so pissed off?

                         WALTER

Those rich fucks! This whole fucking thing—I did
not watch my buddies die facedown in the muck so
that this fucking *strumpet*—

                          DUDE

I don't see any connection to Vietnam, Walter.

                         WALTER

Well, there isn't a literal connection, Dude.

                          DUDE

Walter, face it, there isn't *any* connection. It's
your roll.

                         WALTER

Have it your way. The point is—

                          DUDE

It's your roll—

                         WALTER

The fucking point is—

                          DUDE

It's your roll.

                      VOICE (O.S.)

Are you ready to be fucked, man?

138

They both look up.

Quintana, on his way out, looks down at them from the lip
of the lanes. Over his polyester all-in-one he now wears a
windbreaker with a racing stripe and "Jesus" stitched on
the breast. He is holding a fancy black-and-red leather
ball satchel (perhaps a Sylvia Wein). Behind him stands his
partner, O'BRIEN, a short fat Irishman with tufted red
hair.

> QUINTANA

> I see you rolled your way into the semis. Dios
> mio, man. Seamus and me, we're going to fuck you
> up.

> DUDE

> Yeah well, that's just, ya know, like, your opin-
> ion, man.

Quintana looks at Walter.

> QUINTANA

> Let me tell you something, pendejo. You pull any
> your crazy shit with us, you flash a piece out on
> the lanes, I'll take it away from you and stick it
> up your ass and pull the fucking trigger till it
> goes "click."

> DUDE

> Jesus.

> QUINTANA

> You said it, man. Nobody fucks with the Jesus.

esus walks away. Walter nods sadly.

> WALTER

> . . . Eight-year-olds, Dude.

hroughout the time that *The Big Lebowski* was being filmed on the bowling alley set, but specifically during those sometimes extended periods between set-up changes, it was not uncommon to find Joel off by himself, quietly channeling the Old Guy in the Pro Shop, whom he had met the first time they checked out the Hollywood Star Lanes on Santa Monica Boulevard as a possible location. "You wouldn't believe the things that go on in bowling," Joel–cum–Old Guy in the Pro Shop would say in an ominous, laconic, gravel-pitty voice. Then he would run down the short but nonetheless striking list of things you wouldn't believe: "Bribery. Extortion. *Murder* . . . !

"No one," Joel the Old Guy would summate, "has done the real story of bowling!"

Indefatigable repetition of such encountered character gems is something both Coens have a proclivity toward, though as he's matured, Ethan, in this rarely studied phenomenon of Coenian self-entertainment, has taken more to crooning bars from his favorite country-and-western songs. Each time I heard Joel evoke the spirit of the Old Guy in the Pro Shop, though, I would marvel admiringly at the restraint and maturity it must have taken for him not to accept the coot's portentous challenge to his credulity and counter with "Oh, yeah? Well, how 'bout pederasty? Is there pederasty in bowling?!"

Because a pederast is exactly what the Coens decided to make the Dude and Walter's arch bowling nemesis, Jesus Quintana, bestowing upon him a criminal record for exposing himself to an eight-year-old, and thereby upping the ante of things that the Old Guy in the Pro Shop would defy us to believe go on in bowling.

The Quintana scene, which immediately follows the great-room scene, is actually a scene within a scene. Its overall objective is the same: to introduce us in high style to the character of Jesus Quintana, the Dude, Walter, and Donny's main concern in their drive toward the league championships. As they watch Jesus' bowling form from their own lane, and perhaps in an effort to defuse fear through moral superiority, Walter reveals to the Dude Quintana's past scrape with the laws of man and God. In a brazen ly intrusive flashback, Walter's voice-over narration recounts how Quintana, upon his release from prison and his relocation to Venice, had to go door-to-door to tell his new neighbors that he was a pederast. It is a wacky jack-in-the-box scene reminiscent of the tailor flashback in *The Hudsucker Proxy*, where Sidney Mussburger is saved from the certain death of self-defenestration via Norville Barnes's quick hands and the stitching of his trousers.

As we return to the bowling alley, the Dude tells Walter of the $20,000 fee he will earn for handing the $1 million over to the kidnappers, and proudly notes, as though it were the fruit of cagey negotiating on his part, that he will also retain the unbespattered Lebowski rug. As they idly conjecture about the kidnapping, Walter, springboarding cannonball-style from an offhanded conjecture of the Dude's, suddenly and angrily concludes that Bunny Lebowski's kidnapping is a fraud that she has engineered herself. Which, of course, brings him, suddenly and angrily, to the subject of Vietnam. Finally, Quintana and his teammate, on their way out, stop at the Dude and Walter's lane for some posturing and taunting about the upcoming semifinals.

JOEL   "Quintana was an early element in the script, and we knew that we wanted John Turturro to play him. As we did subsequent drafts of the script, though, we decided we wanted to give him something a little more meaty to sink his teeth into than, you know, just playing this bowling nemesis who happens to be pretty good.

"I had seen him about ten years ago in a play at the Public Theater called *Ma Puta Vita*, in which he played a pederast. Well, maybe that's taking it a little too far, saying he was a pederast—but he had a scene where there was this little boy on his lap and he was kind of bouncing him up and down, and there was kind of a lewd section with weird overtones. I was very impressed with it.

"So we thought, well, let's make Turturro a pederast. It'll be something he can really run with. I guess you could say it's just

Ethan and Joel with John Turturro.

our attempt to bring John's *Ma Puta Vita* character to a wider audience.

"As Ethan and I talked about it, we decided—you know, with Megan's Law and all that stuff—that we'd do the little thing where he had to go door-to-door and tell everyone he's a pederast. Though I don't think pederasts actually have to do that, go door-to-door and ring bells that way, tell people they're pederasts.

"The costume he wears was established pretty early on. We actually wrote that into the script, probably in the first draft. We wanted him to be a real sharp dresser. And when we went to various bowling alleys to look for locations, we kept seeing people with these big bionic hands—big plastic wrist-support things that looked sort of Darth Vaderish. We thought that would be good for a pederast to wear, so we put him in one of those.

"We shot a lot of his stuff in extreme slow motion. It's a scene that starts from their point of view—Dude, Walter, and Donny's—with the three discussing his pederasty while watching him bowl. And you want to isolate that moment, isolate wh.

they're looking at in a way that stands out from the rest of the movie.

"The Quintana scene was fun to do. We haven't done a movie with Turturro in a long time."

ETHAN "Quintana's the bad guy, but he's a minor character, so we made him pretty broad. The main guys, the Dude and Walter, their characters are sort of schlubs, and Quintana, he's like the Jack Palance character—the gunslinger, the slick guy. His ball satchel matches his jumpsuit. He's all coordinated. And, of course, there was the pederast wrist-support thing. I'm not sure why we decided to make him a pederast. But it's good, don't you think?

"We wanted to shoot Quintana in a slow-motion montage sequence, to introduce his nemesis character with the appropriately heightened drama. There's a really good Gypsy Kings cover of the Eagles song 'Hotel California' that we hope to play over it.

"We also did a bunch of slow-motion stuff around that time not specifically for the Quintana scene, but for a credit sequence. Again, a montage-type thing. Slow-motion balls hitting pins, people bowling—you know, the Olympic thing. We never really got the Holy Grail of those kinds of shots—that, of course, being a person's face jiggling all over the place—but we did get some stuff of a guy with a big round gut. It didn't swish back and forth or anything, because it had too much muscle in it. Still, it looks pretty good.

"Inserting the flashback of Quintana going door-to-door in the middle of the scene we did because, stylistically, it's just kind of a wild leap. It's not part of the rest of the movie. It's an accent in the same sense that the metal-flake blue is an accent in the bowling alley, against all that orange and cream."

ΘGER "They had storyboarded a lot of high-speed—slow-motion—work, so you needed a lot more light than you would normally. It's an old bowling alley and there was no light source there. It lights up, but there wasn't enough to film by. So the whole place, basically, we redesigned the lighting in. We had it all rerigged, with fast fluorescents, which took a couple of weeks. Every actual light in the bowling alley we put in there.

"Fluorescent lights usually have a magnetic ballast that regulates the flow of current in the circuit. When you put in an electronic ballast, it's basically pulsing at an incredibly high frequency and is a much brighter light source. So it all had to be changed into those kind of tubes. It was a huge rig. We had fast fluorescents in the actual lanes themselves and over the sitting areas and the scoreboard areas. It was a lot of money and a lot of time invested in rerigging the bowling alley, but when we came to shoot in it, I didn't really have to do much, because it was pre-lit.

"Except for the neon stars. Rick made these neon stars to go on the building's exterior that he turned around and used on the interior wall as well, with the neon then facing the wall and creating a nice kind of silhouetted effect. They looked great, but the trouble was they were neon and you can only shoot neon at certain frame speeds, otherwise it pulses on the film. So for the shots in which we wanted to do a speed change, we had to angle the camera in such a way as to keep the neon stars out of the shot, or otherwise use a camera speed where they wouldn't flicker.

"The street scene, with Quintana going door-to-door, was nice, I thought, with Griffith Park and those huge palm trees. It was kind of a seedy neighborhood that wasn't like a postcard shot. But that was mainly about picking the right look of the location."

RICK   "The bowling alley stars we built ourselves. They wer foam. We painted them silver first, then sprayed this blue in mixed with glitter on top of that. It was really hard to achiev because after a certain amount of ink, it no longer reflects glitt back at you, so we had to be sure that it just reached that point and no further. They have a little sparkle to them now.

"I wanted the blue of the stars backlit with a very cool light against all the orange. It really needed that accent on the wall. It was a natural for neon. I didn't even consider incandescent. Incandescent is a very warm light.

"In the beginning, Roger was concerned that the backlighting on the stars wouldn't show up, so it's not something he really used. We went ahead with it anyway, and it turned out it was plenty visible and I was glad we did it. And Roger graciously said, 'No, it looks great.'

"Of course, nobody knew about the pulsing business.

"Neon is a gas that is electrified. It's not a filament, which is what incandescent is. Neon works on a ballast that runs electricity through it at a certain number of cycles. They were shooting high-speed, which is anything over twenty-four frames per second. Neon works at sixty cycles, which meant there was a pulsing unless you shot at certain frame rates. Any scene in which they wanted the backlit stars couldn't be shot faster than sixty frames per second. Now if we'd found something that pulsed at one hundred and twenty cycles, we would have been fine. We couldn't find anything, but we certainly checked it out. So, that was a downside."

MARY "It was written in the script that Jesus Quintana was in a one-piece stretchy polyester jumpsuit with the name Jesus stitched on it. We made him totally matching, with his jumpsuit matching his jacket and his shoes and these sleazy see-through nylon socks. The prop guys went out and got his ball satchel dyed to match the outfit. And John Turturro came up with the idea that Quintana should have a long pinky fingernail. So Jean Black, the makeup supervisor, got swatches of the fabric we were using and found nail polish that matched.

"In doing research for the movie, we came across the fact that there are these rings you can get for scoring a fully striked game.

There is a 300 ring, a 299 ring, and there is an 800 ring for bowling three consecutive high-scoring games. So we gave Quintana a few of those.

"I felt Quintana's jumpsuit should be really tight, because he is a pervert. And the way John is built, it would emphasize the little dance that he does with his hips, and he needs to look really kind of sleazy. It's almost like a '70s jumpsuit, except we didn't bell the pants. We tried a looser one, but it was totally different. It looked much more like Jim Nabors on *The Andy Griffith Show*—much more wholesome, with a lower crotch. But when he put on the older '70s-type jumpsuit and it was really tight—it was instantly Jesus.

"We had to be really careful with the colors, because you didn't want it to blend in, you wanted it to stand out in a flamboyant, Hispanic way. There were certain colors I really wanted to stay away from. I didn't want it to be the colors in the bowling alley. And there are certain colors that if made into a jumpsuit automatically look like a uniform, such as anything in the forest-green family or sage-green family. And there are a lot of gas stations that use navy or red. So I picked colors that were not on the primary palate—mauve, teal, etc. They're more secondary colors—secondary, but saturated.

"There was another element that we didn't end up using, and that was a penis enhancement we made out of birdseed encased in a thin, stretchy fabric. It was in the shape of a penis. I had a mock-up of one for my meeting with John. He put it down there and really liked it because it helped boost the effect when he thrust his hips forward.

"He wore it for the flashback scene, but when he had it on under his jumpsuit, Joel said, 'Jesus, this is really obscene.' He felt that it might be the thing that tipped us over into NC-17, because the jumpsuit was so tight, it made the fake penis very visible. I'm glad he didn't end up wearing it. It would have been too much.

"It's a trick I've used before, though. If you ever want somebody to look like an old man, give him really big balls. And yo can make big balls out of birdseed and stretchy fabric. They droop just like big balls do.

"And, also, you know, his underwear was perfect. He wore low-rise briefs—bikini underwear for men—because I felt it was the kind of underwear Jesus would wear and I wanted that kind of panty line if it showed. I don't know if anybody realized they were there, but John loved it because it helped him get into the character, and I loved it because I'm obsessed and it gave me a cheap little thrill.

"For the flashback scene, where he's ringing doorbells, I dressed him in those stretch jeans that you buy at JCPenney. And a lot of guys who wear them wear them pressed. But it was also in the script that he had pressed jeans and a tight sweater. I did what the script said.

"I definitely wanted him to be in ones that were snug, and fit him the same way that his jumpsuit fit him. And we definitely wanted an open neck, because there is something about having a closed neck that somehow, on John Turturro at least, immediately cleaned him up and made him look not so sleazy. So an open neckline was good.

"Then we gave him that Jesus necklace that he wore. Originally I thought he would only wear that in the flashback, implying that he always had to have something on his body that said his name. But Ethan and Joel really liked it and said to leave it on, so we did."

There are a few minor storyboard oddities worth mentioning here. One is that the close-up of Quintana's stitched-on name is transposed from left to right in its evolution from thumbnail sketch to film—evidence that supports J. Todd's keen though useless observation that Joel and Ethan visualize things the same, but reversed. In the storyboard of the flashback insert, the unavailability of a recent photo of John Turturro resulted in J. Todd's depiction of not Jesus Quintana ambling up the walk to ring a doorbell and relate his sexual history, but the character of Barton Fink. And finally, in the set-up immediately following that one (set-up #19-4), as he gazes into the eyes of his burly, beer-swilling, TV-sports-watching, underwear-bedecked neighbor, Barton Fink has metamorphosed into Ethan during his cigarette-smoking days, inexplicably sporting an Ace Ventura haircut.

Chapter 11

The Corvette-Smashing Scene

Canned Art

Scene 52

EXT. RESIDENTIAL AREA—LARRY'S HOUSE—NIGHT

Walter is striding down the lawn with his attaché case like
an enraged encyclopedia salesman.

> WALTER
> Fucking language problem, Dude.

e pops the Dude's trunk, flings in the briefcase, and takes
ut a tire iron.

                    WALTER (CONTINUING)
        . . . Maybe he'll understand this.

He is walking over to the Corvette.

                    WALTER (CONTINUING)
        . . . YOU SEE WHAT HAPPENS, LARRY!

CRASH! He swings the crowbar into the windshield, which
shatters.

                    WALTER (CONTINUING)

        . . . YOU SEE WHAT HAPPENS?!

CRASH! He takes out the driver's window.

                    WALTER (CONTINUING)
        THIS IS WHAT HAPPENS WHAT YOU FUCK A STRANGER IN
        THE ASS!

Lights are going on in houses down the street. Distant dogs
bark.

                    WALTER (CONTINUING)
        . . . HERE'S WHAT HAPPENS, LARRY!

CRASH!

                    WALTER (CONTINUING)
        . . . HERE'S WHAT HAPPENS! FUCK A STRANGER IN THE
        ASS!

CRASH!

A MAN in a sleeveless T-shirt and boxer shorts has run over
behind Walter and grabbed him from behind on a backswing of
the crowbar.

                        MAN

    150

WHAT THE FUCK JOO DOING, MANG?!

He wrestles the crowbar away from the startled Walter.

                    MAN
      I JUS' BAWDEEZ FUCKEEN CAR LASS WEEK!

Walter cringes before the enraged Mexican.

                    WALTER
      . . . Hunh?

The man looks about, wildly.

                    MAN
      I KILL JOO, MAN! I—I KILL JOR FUCKEEN CAR!

He runs over to the Dude's car.

                    DUDE
      No! No! NO! THAT'S NOT—

CRASH! CRASH!

                    MAN
      I FUCKEEN KILL JOR FUCKEEN CAR!

CRASH!

                    MAN (CONTINUING)
      . . . I KILL JOR FUCKEEN CAR!

INSIDE THE CAR

Glass rains in on a terrified, cringing Donny.

                    MAN
      I KILL JOR FUCKEEN CAR!

The Corvette-smashing scene is the climax to the overall arc of the homework-in-the-Baggie story, an arc that must be retraced here in order to fully appreciate its climax.

The Dude's car has been stolen from the bowling alley parking lot, and with it the briefcase containing the $1 million in ransom money that the Big Lebowski gave him for delivery to Bunny Lebowski's kidnappers, a delivery that the Dude, thanks largely to Walter's commando-style histrionics, miserably botched.

The Dude's car is soon recovered by the police, but without the briefcase in its trunk. However, wedged between the seats, the Dude finds an object left behind by the joyriders who took the car: ninth-grader Larry Sellers's theme paper on the Louisiana Purchase.

Walter does a background check and learns that Larry Sellers lives in North Hollywood and is the progeny of Arthur Digby Sellers, the head writer for the 1960s Chuck Connors TV show *Branded*, a little bit of history that greatly excites the excitable vet.

As the Dude and Walter drive up to the Sellerses' modest North Hollywood residence, the Dude is upset to see a shiny new red Corvette parked out front, and profanely voices his concern that little Larry has already spent the briefcase's contents.

Once inside, the sleuthing bowlers find the former head writer for *Branded* pajamaed, enfeebled, and lying somewhat anachronistically in a fully functioning iron lung that dominates his home's tiny living-room area.

After paying a brief and moving homage to the metallically enclosed scenarist, Walter confronts little Larry with his embaggied theme paper: "Is this your homework, Larry?" The question is repeatedly put to the taciturn teen, whose sullenness seems to be trumping Walter's bombast in an epic battle of wills. When even evocations of Vietnam fail to draw a reaction, Walter rises and suggests that little Larry watch through the front window. As he exits Walter pauses dramatically to intone: "This is what happens when you FUCK a STRANGER in the ASS, Larry."

Which brings us to the climactic Corvette-smashing scene.

ETHAN "We really liked the line 'This is what happens when you fuck a stranger in the ass.' And, you know . . . it's just . . . you know . . . . Boy. It's hard. What do you say about this? It's one scene built around a really stupid gag.

"The only problem was that John [Goodman] was particularly sensitive about his very distinct and very recognizable voice screaming 'This is what happens when you fuck a stranger in the ass' in the middle of this neighborhood at three in the morning because we hadn't put up any of the neighbors in hotels. Oddly, nobody seemed to mind. And people whose houses we needed access to, or who we asked to do stuff, you know, like move their cars, we paid. We'd wake a guy up in the middle of the night and say, 'Here's a quarter.'"

JOEL "It was pretty straightforward, really. There wasn't anything too complicated. Just keeping bits of glass and fiberglass off of Goodman. That was the only real challenege—not getting him cut up. Yeah. Everyone likes to see a Corvette smashed."

ROGER "This was a location where I felt the street was too wide. The street exterior location was the actual exterior of the house we used for the interior location in the preceding scene. They didn't have to be connected, really. You could have cheated and split them up. But it was nice that the windows were the same on the exterior and interior and you didn't have to worry about them much. So it was good to do the exterior at the same place you do the interior, right?" He laughs.

"But the street was quite wide. It was tree-lined and you didn't get a sense of the neighborhood very much. It didn't lend itself to crosslight—you know, different houses being lit and different lights out front. It was very dark. So, actually, I didn't do a lot on this. I kept it very, very simple and just did it through the suggestion of a couple of streetlights on either side of the street, basically using them as crosslight for the whole scene.

"There was a streetlight opposite the house and initially it seemed that the obvious thing to do would be to make that streetlight the source. So I hung a couple of lights up there, thinking that's what I was going to do. I was hoping to do a kind of pool of light and let it drop off, and when they drove up, they'd be right under it. But I didn't like it, so I took them down. It was too flat, basically. It looked posed, as well. Too well lit.

"So then I just decided to crosslight from down the length of the street. I took a streetlight source on one side of the street and one on the other and crossed the light diagonally. But there were trees and one of those trees prevented one streetlight from actually crossing the other. So when the actors would move from the front of the house across the street to where the Dude's car was parked, they would go through a light that came from the right, and then as they went into the street, that light from the right would be shaded by a tree and they would come into a light from the left that was then coming out from behind another tree. So it was like a crosslight, but the two lights didn't interfere with each other.

"Now, when we got to some of the close-ups, for some of the shots I needed more light on the house in the background, and I had to move the crane that had the light on it around to bring that light onto the house. But by moving that light and putting it on the house, it put light into the street where I didn't want it. So the guys you saw running around with bits of trees on stands were actually replacing where the tree was to keep light off the street. They were cutting the light off where I didn't want it to be and giving a tree pattern on the actual surface of the road where we were looking down and seeing it. A lot of lighting is about taking it away, not putting it on.

"Getting the orange streetlight effect here was tricky, because we had HMI lamps instead of tungsten lights for that set-up. HM lamps are daylight-balanced and tungsten lights interior night. To make a street scene orange, it would have been better to use tungsten lights, because they're warmer to start with.

"But you try to keep the package of lighting down as much as possible. So we ended up using big HMI lamps because we had them with us, and we just put gels in front of them—they had so much gel in front of them. HMI lamps are also very hot and they quickly burned through the gels. So that was a bit of a pain."

RICK   "There's not really a whole lot I can say about this, except it's really exciting. There's nothing in a scene like this that requires my attention. But I love the scene because it's really funny.

"The neighborhood was a big deal to figure out, in terms of the look. That was something Joel and Ethan were kicking back and forth. Originally, I thought it was going to be more of a Valley neighborhood. I thought it would be nice to see some real downwardly mobile San Fernando Valley–looking suburb with scorched lawns. But I think Joel and Ethan perceived it as a nicer place. I think they probably realized it was a good scene and that it didn't matter all that much where it was.

"The other thing was just knowing the fact that the actors were going to be screaming curse words in the middle of the night. I mean, it's an awfully nice neighborhood."

MARY   "I didn't want Walter's suit to look like an expensive or sophisticated one, which is why I went for brown instead of navy or gray, which to me are a little bit more sophisticated. We made the suit ill-fitting, as though he'd probably put on a few pounds in the ten years since he'd bought the suit, but still continued wearing it.

"His suit was pretty new-looking when we got it, so we had to age it a lot. We sanded it and dirted it up a bit. We wanted to make it look old and sort of pilling. We added a lot of water to try

155

to get it to droop a bit, so that the shoulders were a bit fucked-up and crinkly. With Walter, we'd always stretch out his pockets, because he carries things in them. Like with his vest, he has a flashlight and a lighter and his cigarettes and stuff, so there are permanent stretch marks in his vest for those things. We did the same thing with his suit. We dampened the fabric and literally put heavy weights in the pockets along with the objects we wanted to shape them into, then left it for three nights or so.

"His shirt, well, it was just sort of a bad Sears shirt. It's not one he spends a lot of money on. It's just an ecru dress shirt that you buy for fifteen ninety-nine and it is sixty percent poly and forty percent cotton. The tie we thrifted—purchased from a thrift store. The tie was the only thing of John's we thrifted, since it was the same size tie as anyone else's tie. The shirt, and everything else for John, we couldn't thrift because of his size.

"An interesting thing to me is that he has a T-shirt underneath his dress shirt. It looks like it comes from his childhood, like his mom told him this is how you wear it—when you wear a suit you should have a dress shirt and a tie and suit, and you wear a T-shirt under your dress shirt.

"For Luis Colina, who plays the Corvette owner, the script says he comes out in his underwear and a sleeveless T-shirt. For some reason, I always felt like there needed to be something else for that character, since he does own a Corvette. I know Luis from *Hudsucker*, on which he was an editor, and I knew he had an Hispanic accent, so that gave us the idea of a guayabera shirt, which is a lounging button shirt with pleats and embroidery.

"We dressed him as though he had come home and unbuttoned his guayabera shirt, which maybe he'd been wearing during the day with a T-shirt underneath, and then got out of his pants, under which he'd been wearing boxers. In talking about his shoes, Joel said to Luis, 'Oh, yeah, you should have wing tips on.' But we ended up using a snazzier street shoe, like somebody who drives a Corvette might own. He's just kind of in this relaxed mode and this guy has just woken him up out of a slumber and he is pissed. He's still wearing his dress socks and he slipped his dress shoes back on before going out the door. But basically, he's in his underwear.

"Now, you see Larry Sellers staring out the window, watching, so I'll talk about him. This is a good example of me being completely off-base. Initially one of my ideas for the whole scene was that they'd been woken up. The Dude and Walter have come over and it is late enough that the Sellers family are all in their pajamas. And Joel and Ethan said, 'No, we don't want it to be that late.'

"Then, in my initial fitting with the kid, I made him too soft and suburban, like just a normal kid. And Joel and Ethan said, 'He's a smart-ass. He steals cars. You have to make him look like more of a smart-ass.' So I had to refit him and we made him a 'wannabe,' a suburban kid trying to look like an urban hip-hop kid.

"He ended up in jeans that were big bells. I frayed them, cut the bottoms off, but made them really long as though he's always stepping on them. And big honkin' basketball shoes and a T-shirt and an open plaid shirt. Right now wearing plaid is probably a little passé, but at the time the movie takes place, it was probably the hipper thing.

"And Joel and Ethan were happy with that. But that's a good example of me interpreting the character wrong."

The Corvette-smashing scene, despite it's simplicity—or perhaps because of it—is vintage Coen. It involves, via the choice of non-diminutive film editor Luis Colina in the role of the Corvette owner, not one but *two* sequential acts of destruction by *two* howling fat men, making it, at least mathematically, the most ambitious and laughter-intense Howling Fat Man scene the Coens have done, capping a career that brims with howling fat men.

The only other movie in which the Coens have been brazen enough to put two howling fat men on screen simultaneously is *Raising Arizona,* at the moment when Gale and Evelle Snopes realize they've left behind Gale/Nathan Jr., and seconds later, an ink bomb hidden in money recently stolen from a bank explodes in a blue fury. In *The Big Lebowski*'s Corvette-smashing scene, however, the Coens not only push open the envelope and climb the pyramid of Howling Fat Mandom, they cojoin the motif with another Coen comic mainstay—the imbecilic phrase that is endlessly repeated and thereby milked for cheap laughs quite nearly to the point of desiccation (or as Ethan might say, beaten to death). That the Coens, at this point in their career, would combine two such motifs, one of which itself is already doubled, stands in testament to their creativity's bounty.

Well. That, or its poverty.

But the important thing is, it stands in testament.

For the filming of the Corvette-smashing scene, there were actually two shiny new red Corvettes used, all so that extra camera coverage could be attained of the Corvettes' windows being smashed. The sports cars were not purchased outright for the scene; rather, they were rented with the understanding that the sports cars' shells would be damaged and replaced, but the engines and chassis of the vehicles would remain unscathed.

During filming, the inevitable, of course, occurred: a police squad car came by to check on a report of vandalism in the vicinity. One never knows if this sort of thing is the legitimate tip of a concerned citizen or the revenge-motivated prank of a sleepless, grainy-eyed neighbor who has suddenly realized how deeply he undersold his capacity for annoyance.

Storyboard-wise, Joel's comments regarding J. Todd Anderson's helpful extracurricular areas of knowledge can be viewed firsthand in his modest notation that a Corvette's headlights must first be "popped up" before they can be smashed. Also note the bunny slippers with which J. Todd has beshoed the Corvette owner, a point that could be missed in the more dominant and puzzling feature of the Corvette owner's resemblance to one of the guys convicted of the World Trade Center bombing.

Chapter 12

Busby Berkeley Dream Sequence

The Legend of the Ugly Tile Floor, Part 2

Scene 57

NT. DREAM SEQUENCE #2—NIGHT

cratchy white title card:

        JACKIE TREEHORN PRESENTS

other title card:

        THE DUDE

AND

MAUDE LEBOWSKI

IN

A third title card:

GUTTERBALLS

The title logo is a suggestively upright bowling pin flanked
by a pair of bowling balls. The bending bass sound turns
into the lead-in to Kenny Rogers and the First Edition's
"JUST DROPPED IN."

The Dude is walking down a long corridor dressed as a cable
repairman. The Dude's face is washed with a brilliant light
as the corridor opens onto a gleaming bowling alley.

In the center of the alley stands Maude Lebowski, singing
operatic harmony to the Kenny Rogers song. She wears an
armored breastplate and Norse headgear, has braided pig-
tails, and holds a trident.

The Dude stands behind her and, pressed up against her,
help her with her follow-through as she releases a bowling
ball.

The lane is straddled by a line of chorines in spangly
miniskirts, their arms akimbo, Busby Berkeley—style, their
legs turning the lane into a tunnel leading to the pins at
the end.

But it is no longer a bowling ball rolling between their
legs—it is the Dude himself, levitating inches off the
lane, the tools from his utility belt swinging free. He is
facedown, his arms, torpedolike, pressed against his sides

His point of view shows the lane rushing by below, the lit

tle ball-guide arrows zipping by.

The Dude twists his body around, performing a barrel roll so that he is now gliding along the lane faceup.

Now his point of view looks up the dresses of the passing chorines.

The Dude smiles dreamily and does a backstroke motion so that he is once again gliding facedown. He looks forward and his forward momentum blows back his hair.

Coming at us, as we go through the last few pairs of legs, are the approaching pins. We hit the pins, scattering them, and rush on into the black.

A body drops down into the blackness in slow motion — a topless woman, squealing, her legs kicking.

As she drops out of frame, leaving blackness again, three men are entering from the background, emerging into a pool of light. It is the Germans, advancing ominously, wielding oversized shears which they menacingly scissor.

The Dude, now standing in a field of black, reacts to the advancing Germans. He turns and runs, fists pumping.

T he Busby Berkeley dream sequence is the second and larger of the two dream sequences generated by the abruptly unconscious mind of the Dude. But as the two dreams are connected thematically, if not representationally, some mild indulgence in plot exposition regarding the Lebowski Dream Cycle, if we may call it that, is appropriate.

The first dream sequence occurs when the Dude, lying peacefully upon the urine-free rug acquired from the Lebowski mansion and listening through headphones to tapes of the Venice Beach League play-offs, 1987, is suddenly sapped across the chin by a mystery woman and her male attendant. The mystery woman is Maude Lebowski, estranged Fluxus artist daughter of the Big Lebowski; she wants the rug, which was a gift from her to her late mother. All of this is more or less foretold in the first dream sequence. Featuring a lot of digital special effects to the strains of Bob Dylan's "The Man in Me," dream sequence #1 depicts the Dude flying over the L.A. area as, ahead of him, Maude, whom he doesn't yet know beyond his brief preconcussive sighting of her, rides away on the now magically flying rug. A bowling ball appears in the Dude's hand, ending with Newtonian rigor his experiment in flight, and depositing him in a bowling alley, where, now tiny and trapped inside the thumbhole of a bowling ball, the Dude is rolled down a lane by the woman he soon will know, both Biblically and nomenclaturally, as Maude.

That's the first dream sequence. We could've done a chapter on that one instead, but you would've had nothing to look at but pictures of Jeff Bridges dangling in front of a blue screen. Be thankful you're in the hands of competent people.

The second, or so-called Busby Berkeley, dream sequence, with which this chapter is concerned, occurs some time later. By this point in the story the Dude has met Maude Lebowski, who has informed him that the $1 million her father gave him as ransom money for Bunny, which we and the Dude know is missing, was in fact embezzled by her father from the Little Lebowski Urban Achievers Foundation, of which Maude and her father are the sole trustees.

Not wishing to call the police in on family matters, yet convinced that the kidnapping is a scam perpetrated by Bunny, Maude hires the Dude to recover the money from the kidnappers, to whom she thinks the Dude has paid the ransom, promising the Dudester a $100,000 finder's fee for his trouble. For the Dude's edification, Maude shows him a porn video entitled *Logjammin'*, produced by smut king Jackie Treehorn and starring Bunny Lebowski and her nihilist pal Uli. It is a wooden sex romp depicting a cable repairman's visit to a young woman's apartment during shower time.

Also by this point in the story, the Dude has gotten a visit from Uli himself, in the company of his fellow nihilists and former band mates. Professing to be the kidnappers, they destroy the Dude's answering machine with a cricket paddle, then toss a marmot into the bathtub with him and demand that he cough up their ransom money by the next day or they will cut off his penis. And then stomp on it. And squish it.

Right.

So, then: at the point when the Busby Berkeley dream sequence finally arrives, the Dude has just been dragged to the beach home of smut king Jackie Treehorn, who wants to know where Bunny is, because of her sizable financial debt to him. Treehorn offers the Dude a drink, and a ten percent finder's fee to recover the debt.

By way of answer the Dude collapses, Mickey-Finned.

And dreams his second dream of the movie.

It starts with title cards introducing a Jackie Treehorn production called *Gutterballs* that stars the Dude and Maude Lebowski. As the dream begins, Kenny Rogers and the First Edition perform "Just Dropped In" on the sound track. The Dude, wearing Uli's cable repairman costume from *Logjammin'*, dances onto a barren concrete dreamscape, the enormous shadow cast by his tiny form jiving across and quickly consuming a craggy cement wall as he approaches.

Suddenly, the Dude is stepping up to a rental bowling shoe rack that stretches up to the moon. Working the rental counter this night is Saddam Hussein, who offers a special pair of bowling shoes to His Dudeness.

And suddenly, the Dude is dancing in the bowling shoes down the steps of a stairway to infinity, onto a magical bowling lane, where a line of chorines backs up Maude, who awaits the Dude, dressed like a Norse goddess majestically brandishing a trident. The chorines dance, and there ensues a quasi-erotic bowling lesson between the Dude and Maude, as he steps up behind her and they go through the motions, so to speak. They toss the bowling ball and it rolls down an impossibly long bowling lane between the legs of the straddling chorines.

Only, it's not the bowling ball—it's the Dude who's going down the lane between the legs of the chorines. Floating above the maple, the Dude rotates, looks happily up the chorines' skirts, and then crashes into the bowling pins for a strike.

In the abyssal dark, a bare-breasted woman we recognize from a blanket toss at Jackie Treehorn's beach party rises and falls again. And suddenly, the three nihilists emerge from the black, clacking scissors menacingly. The Dude turns in fear. And runs . . .

Busby Berkeley, the dream sequence's namesake, was an unschooled but ingeniously innovative choreographer from the early days of American musical cinema. He is credited with being the first film choreographer to use the camera's mobility and the editing potential of celluloid to provide a perspective to dance routines impossible to experience in a traditional stage setting. It is Busby Berkeley, for example, who first used the high overhead shot on chorus dance routines to create kaleidoscopic patterns out of the dancers' bodies.

But as much as Berkeley was known for filmic innovation, he was also famous for his unbridled deco gaudery and unabashedly kitschy style. Long lines of chorines playing neon violins, chorines dressed as giant coins—Busby was, simply put, irrepressible.

It is with Busby Berkeley in mind that the Coens' second dream sequence in *The Big Lebowski* was conceived, with a heavily stylized set, drawing largely from a black-and-white palette so as to suggest the look of a Berkeley-choreographed film.

JOEL   "The Busby Berkeley dream sequence was completely different from anything we've ever done before. We'd done a big dance number with the whole USO thing in Barton Fink, working with the same choreographers, Bill and Jacqui Landrum. But that was very different in that it was an actual dance-hall scene. This was a fantasy musical number.

"There were a lot of practical set-building challenges. We didn't have that much money to do it, but we wanted it to have that real sort of high-gloss, MGM-musical look, though, because it's a comedy, it could afford to be a little bit cheapie-looking in parts. In fact, the original idea was to do it on cheesy stage sets. But it got progressively away from that, and became slicker and slicker.

"There were a lot of challenges. There was the whole thing about building these sets with forced perspective: the staircase, the bowling alley. How to do the stars in the background was a big thing. What the movements, the choreography should be.

"We always knew we wanted the Kenny Rogers song. And we knew we wanted the bowling-lesson idea in the actual choreography. And we always knew we wanted him floating through the lights and turning over and looking up the skirts of the chorines.

"The biggest challenge ended up being floating Jeff through their legs—you know, as a visual effect. It's hard to get a big guy spinning under someone's legs without hitting their legs. There's physically not that much room.

"We shot one pass against the blue screen of the chorus girls out on the lane with their legs straddling the lane. Then another element of him on a rotisserie spit that we'd paint the bar out of later. He was literally in a body harness that spun around. We'll try floating him through their legs afterward in a computer. And we always have the option of shrinking him slightly in the computer.

"But there's not much room. We had to find dancers with really long legs and give them high heels. We asked them specifically to choose really tall dancers."

Rick's sketch of the first shot of the dream sequence.

ETHAN   "The first shot is Rick's thing. We were just sort of moping around, wondering, what's the background? What's the set in
the reverse of the shoe rack? We didn't know and just sort of
moped about it, and Rick drew that sketch of Jeff in which he's
really teeny, but casting an enormous shadow, which we used for
the first panel on the storyboards for the scene.

"Rather than doing the set-up live and building a hundred-foot
set, we shot Jeff against a blue screen, then, via visual effects, will
shrink his image and supply the set around him—the set being a
model, like three feet tall, maybe, that's filmed separately.

"We shot Jeff simultaneously using two cameras. The A camera shot Jeff's image to lay into the model footage. But the B camera shot him against the light source to supply a silhouette shape
a shadow, if you will, that could be twisted and manipulated an
funhouse-mirrored by the visual effects guy, Janek Sirrs, to clim
walls and do what shadows do. The point where his feet meet h

own shadow is a little dicey. The visual effects guy has to sync the shadow image to his feet.

"One lighting challenge was how to shoot the stars. We wanted the bowling alley sort of in space. So we wanted stars and lots of them. And there was a lot of moping around and really boring discussions about how the fuck we could do that. But we ended up using Scotch Lite material and this ring around the lens with little light fixtures on it.

"Toplighting the lane and the platform and keeping the light teased off of the floor was a big deal for Roger.

"Everything has its own weird problems. The dancers' hats were a big deal for Mary. We really liked the idea of the whole Carmen Miranda thing. You want those big banana-type head-dresses, but on the other hand, the chorines have to be able to dance. The first thing Mary came up with, which looked great, was just too heavy to move in. That was another session of sitting around moping, not knowing what the fuck to do.

"We talked a lot to Jean Black, the makeup supervisor, about what the chorines should look like, and Jean said, 'These girls should be like the girl next door, right? They're not bowling whores.' Jean's always right. Can't make 'em bowling whores.

"Actually, we wanted dough-faced women, but they don't make them anymore. In Busby Berkeley movies, the dancers are always dough-faced. Kind of puffy, kind of pudgy. But, you know, in California—good luck. All health, fitness, and beauty. They just don't have L.A. dancers who look like that."

ROGER   "The first image, the little figure and the big shadow—everybody's first idea is 'Oh, let's find some location we can do it on.' But when you think about it, there's no way you can create such a stylized shadow from a figure like that and still have that big beam of light coming across the floor. It's like the drawing is a mixture of two kinds of light source. One light source is a tiny little point source, probably about six feet behind the figure, which would give you his shadow. And the other one, the real

167

Rick's sketch of the Great Wall of Shoes.

light source lighting the space, that's something a hundred feet away. The important thing in the image is the stylization of this big shadow. And then you realize it's got to be done in two pieces. The shadow's got to be created through a visual effect.

"We had a lot of this on *Hudsucker,* where we'd have ten people in a room and we'd all discuss how a particular shot should be approached, and whoever came up with the simplest way to do it was the winner.

"With the shoe-rack set-up, though it's not drawn in the storyboard, they eventually decided they wanted the shot to end up disappearing into the heavens and have a moon above it. With something like that, the only thing you have to work out lighting-wise is how to isolate the sky element from the actual shoe rack. And this particular set was in a poky little corner of the hangar where we shot the whole sequence—so again, there's practical considerations.

"With the whole dream sequence, the challenge was 'How can I keep a consistency to the shots and always make it look like he's in limbo?' So I thought, I'll just keep it really simple and do a top source on every situation. So, basically, with the shoe rack, it is that. It's a twelve-by-twelve silk with some lamplight coming through it, and leveled so that the light is even between the top of the shoe rack and where Saddam is down below.

"But that was the case with all of the set-ups—basically, one soft source. It's simple and it's easy. If you've got a black drape all around and it's something like ten feet from the subject, you need a simple way to light the scene that doesn't go onto the black and show you the drape. And if you toplight, you can just hang cuts on the top lights that take the light away within a very short space before it hits the drape.

"It was simple, but it was definitely the biggest rig. We shot the whole dream sequence in an airplane hangar. I put a really big lighting truss up in the ceiling of the hangar for hanging lights that the electricians could walk on and get to without disturbing the set. Normally, you would probably put up a smaller truss just big enough to hang lights on from off a crane, after which you'd take the crane out. And if one of those lamps goes down, you've got to get the crane back in.

"Because this set was so big and there was so much of it we were seeing—and all these black drapes and stars hanging every-where—it would've been too much to expect to be able to move all that out and bring a crane in. That's why it became a bit of an expensive issue. But it paid off, because we did have to go up there.

"The starfield was done with Scotch Lite. It's like a front pro-jection material. So we had to design a little gag for the front of camera that was lightweight enough to allow the camera to remain mobile for the scene. The gag was a little circle, actually, of MI 16s. They're a kind of little light they use in shop windows for display lighting. We made a tiny little ring of these. And it was on a dimmer, so that when we were on a wide shot, we could have it bright, but when you went into a tight close-up, you could dim it down so that it wouldn't affect the lighting on the actor's face.

"With regard to the set-up where he's going between the dancers' legs—there was a funny thing. When we were shooting in the real bowling alley, we had these shots we had to do of the ball rolling down the lane until it hits the pin. We got this little remote-control car, which this company provides. I think it was made to film some stuff in *Home Alone 2*. Basically, it's a little cam-era mounted on a little remote car. It worked fine in the bowling alley, going fast, keeping up with the bowling ball as it went down the lane.

"And I thought, well, I'll use it in the dream sequence to track down the lane under the girls' legs as though it's Jeff's point of view. But the move we needed was so slow, the gearing on the car just wasn't good enough and it wouldn't work. So we reshot it. We put the camera on a pad and got a big pole and pushed i down the lane. You know, the simplest things—an 18mm len and just pushing this camera down the lane with a big pole. An it worked fine.

"There were three kinds of bowling pins we used for the strik in the fantasy bowling lane. For the first wide shot they were about nine inches high and lit with some little practical bulb. And then as we approached them, they became real-size pins. They were also lit internally with little tungsten tube fixtures. And then finally we hit them. Because they had to fly, we couldn't find any way of lighting them internally, so we used the Scotch Lite material on them to make it look like they were lit internally, when really it was lit by the light gag on the camera.

"The nihilists we shot individually—each as a different element. They'll be matted together later. I can't remember now if we shot them in slow motion. If we did, it was only very slightly slow motion. It might be forty frames per second or something."

RICK "Joel and Ethan always wanted the dream sequence to have a forced-perspective set. At one point it was suggested that they could achieve the perspective as a visual effect. The visual effects guy said, 'We can build the set up to a point and do the rest digitally and it'll work out fine.' And I think they really thought about it, but then realized that that's just not the look they wanted. They didn't want it to be smooth and seamless, necessarily. They wanted it to be slightly theatrical. I'm sure they were referencing the Salvador Dalí dream sequence from the Hitchcock film *Spellbound*, which is kind of funky when you see it, but it's also really cool. It's very expressionistic and immediate. And I don't think they wanted to lose the power of that in technique.

"But I felt they needed a little bit of an introduction to the sequence, so I suggested that we open with the giant shadow shot, instead of just going right to the shoe rack. I wanted it to have a kind of German expressionistic feeling. What we're going for is a kind of big concrete look. You've just been at Jackie Treehorn's house, which is this very '50s, very avant-garde, cool-looking, huge concrete deal. So I thought it would be appropriate to open with something reminiscent of where we've just been. It's kind of an urban dreamscape—maybe not urban, but somewhat *Metropolis*-like, the 1926 Fritz Lang movie, where the

whole point is scale. He's tiny, it's big.

"I originally conceived of the shadow as almost pin-shaped, but they're going to go for Jeff dancing in, and that makes sense. First you see the shadow coming in, and then the Dude comes dancing in and the shadow crawls up the wall.

"To further emphasize the forced perspective, we originally wanted the stairway steps to light up as he descends, so that there'd be a 'Wow, there's no way they could have possibly done those little tiny ones at the top—it must really be a million-mile-long stairway!' But we budgeted that and found it to be too expensive. So we just illuminated the sides of the steps, which is actually good, because it ties in better with the illuminated siderails on the bowling lane. The lane itself we couldn't illuminate either, because there was no way to do it and also have the chorines walk down and stand on it without seeing shadows of support structures and all that.

"Originally, it was going to be a black mirrored floor. We couldn't do that because our black Duvateen, the black drapes, only went to a certain height and you might see weird reflections of their tops. So I decided, well, I guess we have to break it up somehow with a pattern.

"And that's where the black-and-white-checkered floor came in.

"Black-and-white check is a very Busby Berkeley, deco-era pattern, which was good for the feel of the dance sequence, but at the same time, it ties in the great-room hallway floor and turns a negative into a positive. It makes it look like the whole black-and-white-checkered floor was intentional.

"I remember when they first saw the floor out on the set, Joel had to say, 'And, of course, we'll put a whole bunch of urinals along this side over here.' The same joke. I think Joel and Ethan were a little skeptical, but I think they also like to play tricks on themselves and their expectations. And they saw the good reasons why we should do it. As I said, you have to kind of embrace reality. I think I used that word with them and they said, 'Well, you embraced it, all right.'

"For the stars, we used Scotch Lite. It's so optically tuned that eighty percent of any light emitted directly from the camera gets reflected right back into the lens and on the film. So instead of stringing lights, which is what most people do with star curtains, we stuck cutout Scotch Lite onto the Duvateen, turning the pieces toward the camera. And we also strung cutout Scotch Lite on black threads connected to battens and tied down—three to four, maybe five at the most on a string. There were three layers of stars. And they put a fan on them and we actually got a little twinkle. When they weren't being used, we put big pieces of blue tape on the threads at eye level so people wouldn't tangle themselves in them. There was a set dresser on set at all times, and one of her jobs was to tend to the lines.

"One thing we learned from the test we did was that a little star goes a long way. You never need to put as many in as you think you do. But the point was to feel like we're floating. That's why we put black on the floor and the stars on the floor, too. It really does feel like there's no real up or down to this place."

MARY "For me, it was definitely the most intense collaboration on the movie in terms of working with the choreographers, trying to make Joel and Ethan happy, make the choreographers happy, and make myself happy.

"Joel had called me before they had even started the project and said that they were interested in there being a Carmen Miranda–type aspect to the chorines, meaning that they definitely wanted them in headdresses. So I watched every Busby Berkeley movie there was to get inspiration. Our approach was with plastic toy pins. It was probably about a hundred or a hundred and fifty bowling pins of three different sizes. It was like a Carmen Miranda fruit-basket headdress. They started out small and it just kind of exploded at the top. It looked great, but when I took the prototype to the choreographers to see if they could work with it, it was too heavy for what they had intended.

"In the end, we decided to make the headdresses flat, as opposed to making them in the round. We tried to keep th explosion motif, but with the bowling pins fanning out. From the front it looked heavy and three-dimensional, but from the side it was thin. Very fanlike. I figured that the lightest-weight material was going to be foam, so I went to somebody who specializes in making foam creations and he built the foam part of the head-dresses. Then we attached them onto skullcaps that were the same color as the rest of the dancers' outfits. Jacqui, the choreographer, had some ideas about how it should look. Between her and myself and the people who were building the skullcaps, we came up with a way to secure the headdresses as best as we possibly could.

"It ended up being a very lightweight headdress. I was really, really happy with how they turned out. And in the long run it worked much better in terms of the way it was choreographed and with the pattern they make in Roger's overhead shot.

"Still, the first day of shooting was not easy. As lightweight as the headdresses were, to have one on for hours and hours, and to have a lot of back-and-forward head movements—I know those girls were miserable in those headdresses. But not as miserable as they could have been. I kept thinking, thank God it didn't end up being the first one. Things often have a way of working themselves out for the better.

"For the chorines' outfits, I looked through a book on bowling that has a lot of bowling paraphernalia and deals with the history of bowling. In it are pictures of '40s pinup girls, kind of Vargas-style pinup drawings, with bowling themes. Like, there's a girl bowling and her bloomers have dropped. Since it was the '40s, you didn't really see anything except for lots of leg. We decided that we wanted the chorines to have the feeling of those bowling pinup girls.

"I wanted to use rayon as the choice of fabric so that the outfits looked more like old bowling-shirt fabric. Choosing the color was important, because I wanted it to have a reference to the '30s and '40s, and the chorines are the first introduction of real color, because Rick made the set a mostly black-and-white palette. We ended up choosing maroon and cream, a yellowy color.

"We wanted the outfits to be sexy, because it is a dream sequence with sexual overtones. I wanted them to also form a graphic pattern with their clothes, in terms of the repetition of movements and the girls moving between one another in dance formation. We ended up using color on one side of their shirts and another color on the other side, so when they move in and out, you've got that visual pattern. I put a one-inch strip at the bottom of their skirts, because I knew from the storyboards there was that shot of Jeff going through the chorines' legs, and it would look really nice with the dancers going down the alley in a sequence of lines.

"A lot of work went into this dream sequence. There were thirty-two dancers, and just getting the fittings was a challenge. They'd been cast early so that we could start the work, but they were cast so far in advance that some of the dancers would get better jobs and leave, and you'd have to refit the outfit for the replacement dancer.

"Every time you did one thing, it affected thirty-two other pieces. So the design choices had to be made very carefully. You don't have the time or the money to have them ripped apart and started over again. They all had to have shoes, and all the shoes had to match. And the belts had to be made. And they all had to have panties, and we had to dye those to match the skirts. And they had to have the right bras underneath so that they all had similar silhouettes—and on and on!

"Now, the Dude's dream clothing is a takeoff on what Uli wore in the *Logjammin'* video when he plays the cable repairman, though actually we determined what Peter Stormare, who plays Uli, was going to wear based on what we wanted Jeff to wear. At first, because Uli is a nihilist and always wears black and because I wanted the clothing to seem impractical since it's a porn video, we were thinking we should give Uli a black coverall for *Logjammin'*. But then we thought that if the background of the Busby Berkeley dream sequence is all black with stars, then what's going to work best is if Jeff is in a white coverall. So then we put Uli in a white coverall, which was a good idea, because was even more impractical than black.

"Uli's coverall we made really tight, raising the crotch so you could see a lot of the outline of his package, as it were, with the front unbuttoned down to his chest. Jeff's version of that outfit was much more Dudelike. It wasn't tight, and fit him in a much looser way, because the rest of the Dude's clothes are loose. We cut the sleeves off both their coveralls and frayed them. You know, for Uli, it was to show he was like some rough guy, but on the Dude it just looks ridiculous.

"We wanted the Dude to have special bowling shoes for the dream sequence. In all of the bowling scenes, everybody else is always dressed as though they made the effort to buy their own pair of bowling shoes, but the Dude always wears shoes with the size on the back, as though he rented them and then just never gave them back. We wanted to continue that into the dream sequence. But we wanted it to be a really spectacular pair. So we made them two-toned silver and gold, with the center toes painted black to match his black workbelt.

"In the storyboard, Saddam Hussein is shown in uniform. But instead of that, we put him in a bowling shirt with his little beret. And instead of having the war medals that he usually has on his beret, we made up a medal that had a bowling pin in the center of it. I don't know if anyone is even going to notice it. Originally, I thought maybe I'd do Saddam Hussein's bowling shirt in camouflage colors. But we didn't want to introduce a whole lot of color until you saw the chorines, so we kept Saddam Hussein in black and white as well.

"In the script it says Maude is in a Norse outfit. I didn't really want her to be in metal. To me, metal is very summer-stock—you know, rusty and clunky. I wanted it more surreal, more bizarre, than that. Also, I knew from the storyboards that there was the bowling-lesson thing, where he comes up behind her and sort of guides her through it, and that was another reason I didn't want it to be stiff, metal armor. It had to be something that would allow a bit more movement.

"I did a bunch of research on different operas, and really on anything for which someone might get dressed up in a getup like this. It was pictorial research. I found this piece I really responded to. It was this very surreal-looking Norse woman, and that's where the idea came from.

"What we did was a foam dress covered in leather, and we painted it a sort of bronzy-gold color to work with Julianne's hair. And then we made her breastplates bowling balls. She holds a trident that we sprayed to match the outfit. The same thing with the hat, which has a lot of repeated motifs from the dress. The end result is very theatrical, but very soft-looking."

Often, if budgetary or scheduling concerns demand it, the Coens find it within their anal-retentive selves to brashly storyboard a scene out of order—though, of course, it is always done with the greater anal-retentive good in mind. This was the case on *Raising Arizona*, says Ethan, in which the action sequences were storyboarded first so as to give then cinematographer Barry Sonnenfeld advance warning on the types of mounts and other camera equipment he would need.

For *The Big Lebowski*, says J. Todd, it was the Dude's two dream sequences that needed to be storyboarded first—a good five months before the rest of the script. The reason was that the Coens were in the process of hammering out the movie's projected budget and needed a firm grasp of how they envisioned the two sequences in order to understand fully the expense each represented.

And get this: so amazingly well honed is the working relationship between Joel and Ethan and J. Todd over the course of six movies now, that the storyboard session for *The Big Lebowski*'s dream sequences was done over the phone and via fax transmission.

You try telephonically explaining to someone the business about the Dude getting tiny and becoming trapped inside the thumbhole of a bowling ball, and see what spits out of *your* fax machine.

. . . And this is assuming you *like* to talk.

Epilogue

Underneath the Hale-Bopp Sky

"I don't care if you're the Pope of
Rome, President of the United States,
or even Man of the Year—something can
always go wrong."
—Loren Visser (M. Emmett Walsh) in *Blood Simple*

*I*n the end, it is impossible to anticipate life completely, no matter how much one may discuss or cogitate it. The things one expects to be hard—and, accordingly, schedules extra time to accomplish and reinforces with backup plans—turn out to be comically easy. And the things one expects to be easy . . . turn out like the Satchel Toss.

It's the first week in March, in the middle of the night, near the town of Piru in Simi Valley, which means we're in the desert, which means it's windy and butt-puckeringly cold. In order to stay warm, I've had to layer several of the summer shirts I brought for my trip to sunny California beneath a cheap down coat purchased the morning before at an army-navy store in Hollywood. The coat being

179

cheap, I am steadily leaking minute feathers that are quickly swept away by the wind to be scattered into the desert's pitiless abyss like . . . well, like money on a budget movie production when things aren't going well. Like, say, tonight on the set of *The Big Lebowski*.

For although tonight, at this hour and this distance from L.A., comet Hale-Bopp is readily discernible to the naked eye, its cosmic glow is being mocked by terrestrial snafu. Along a back road leading up into some hills, on a small ravine bridge whose concrete surface has been rusticked up a bit with an overlay of weathered boards so as to generate that good old-fashioned wood-bridge rumble when vehicles cross it, Joel and Ethan are filming the botched ransom delivery scene. It's not the motorcycle stunt that's causing problems, or the stunt tumble from a moving car, or the car-crashing-into-a-telephone-pole stunt. No, these highly complex set-ups are all on hold, as Joel and Ethan try to get their overeducated craniums around the Satchel Toss.

In the botched ransom delivery scene, Walter joins the Dude on his nocturnal bagman stint, against the kidnappers' explicit instructions. Wearing camouflage and a bandanna, and carting a satchel full of dirty underwear and an Uzi in a brown paper bag, Walter pushes the Dude aside and commandeers his car. Then he reveals to the Dude his brainstorm alternate plan: at the ransom handoff, give the kidnappers not the briefcase with $1 million, but a "ringer"— the satchel with the dirty underwear. That way, they get to keep the entire $1 million for themselves. But what about Bunny? asks the incredulous and irritated Dude. Okay, says Walter, after the phony handoff, we beat the shit out of the kidnappers until they tell us where they're keeping her.

From these auspicious beginnings, things go horribly awry. The kidnappers, calling on a cell phone, tell the Dude they want him not to hand off the ransom money, but to throw it from the moving car as they cross a bridge. At the bridge, as the Dude reaches for the briefcase of money, Walter abruptly tosses out his satchel of undies in a graceful arc, then rolls from the moving car with his Uzi. Walter hurts himself in the roll, the Uzi discharges chaotically in all directions, and the car, with the Dude in it, crashes into a telephone pole

The frightened kidnappers roar up out of the ravine on motorcycles and disappear into the night. The Dude staggers from the car, brandishing the suitcase of money, and vainly tries to call them back. Limping, Walter shrugs off their failure with his usual aplomb. "Fuck it," he says. "Let's go bowling."

So here's the problem for the Coens. They anticipated their every production need for the scene—from the stuntmen to the special effects guys, right down to the crane for the high shot that captures the graceful arc of the satchel as it sails from Walter's forward-swinging arm. From the beginning, they communicated their special Coenesque vision of the scene to all parties, via storyboards and discussions. But what they did not do—what it never even occurred to them to check—was whether, in fact, the laws of physics permitted a human arm hanging out of a car window to toss a satchel forward in such a way that it sails *at all*—let alone in a high, graceful arc. Genuises at advanced planning, the Coens failed to anticipate something that developed many millions of years ago: the human rotator cuff.

But if you really want to be cruel, you could go back a few *billion* years with the observation that it's not the human rotator cuff that they neglected to consider; it's gravity itself.

My point is, you know—they've had plenty of time.

And so it is that, try as he might, the hale and muscular stunt double for John Goodman can get nothing out of his toss, even after the underwear is removed from the satchel. Each time, upon its release, the satchel merely hangs for a millisecond in the air before dropping artlessly to the ground. Again and again the Coens shoot the act, with the stuntman giving it his all. Again and again Roger tries a different way to cheat the shot that later will allow the Coens to fix it through some undetermined editing feat—but they can't get the satchel to clear the top of the picture frame before it falls, even when they try throwing it not forward, but just straight up and back. When they try to fake it by having the stuntman fling his arm in pantomime of a toss, as a guy crouched low and hidden slings the satchel out the driver's window with both hands, the result is so [un]satiable there is only one thing left to do: break for lunch. As they do, Joel says to Roger: "We figure we'll try the crane shot next and see how screwed we really are." Roger laughs uneasily.

At lunch, Joel and Ethan try to think of a way to master the universe and bend gravity to their will. To this end, Joel starts talking crazy. Blue screen, he says. Maybe they should just film the flinging arm and the moving car and then later, set against a blue screen, film the satchel as a different element, sailing in a high, graceful arc, maybe using strings. Ethan merely stares at the center of the table.

Then, a breakthrough. Wondering why a simple Satchel Toss is taking so goddam long, Jeff Bridges sends out a query from his trailer. Told about the war the Coens are waging against the universe, with a flying satchel the spoils, Jeff wonders, "Why don't they just shoot it in reverse?"

Huh.

And so they do.

After lunch, with the camera up on the crane, the stunt guy drives the car backward over the bridge, his arm raised to the sky, then swinging downward as, off-camera, a guy casually standing next to Joel and Ethan flings the satchel in a graceful arc, reaching the driver's window at just the right moment in time.

And just that simply, underneath the vastness of the Hale-Bopp sky, one of the things the Coens anticipated would be easy, turns out . . .

Well . . . it turns out to be easy after all.

When it comes down to it, all processes, really, are found ones—patterns detected after the fact and optimistically labeled to suggest intent. The Coen Process is, more than anything, simply a dynamic character profile the Coens leave behind on every movie they make. That profile reflects their strengths and weaknesses, their neuroses and idosyncrasies, their experiences or lack thereof, their attentiveness to certain details and their obliviousness to others.

I leave you where we began, with Ethan's post-Oscar remark. *Nothing much makes sense. So, you might as well make whatever kind of movie you want. And hope for the best.*